Luna, Luna

Luna, Luna

Creative Writing Ideas from
Spanish, Latin American,
and Latino Literature

Edited by Julio Marzán

Teachers & Writers Collaborative
New York

Luna, Luna: Creative Writing Ideas from Spanish, Latin American, & Latino Literature

Library of Congress Cataloging-in-Publication Data

    Luna, luna : creative writing ideas from Spanish, Latin American, and Latino literature /
        edited by Julio Marzán.
           p.   cm.
        Includes bibliographical references (p.   ).
        ISBN 0-915924-52-8 (alk. paper)
        1. English language--Composition and exercises--Study and
    teaching--United States.   2. Creative writing--Study and teaching--
    United States.   3. Hispanic American literature (Spanish)--Study
    and teaching--United States.   4. Interdisciplinary approach in
    education--United States.   5. Spanish literature--Study and
    teaching--United States.   I. Marzán, Julio, 1946–   .
    LB1576.L836 1997   96-44822
    372.6'23--dc20   CIP

Acknowledgments

This publication was made possible, in part, through support from the Lannan Foundation and the NEA Challenge Program.

Teachers & Writers programs are made possible, in part, through support from the National Endowment for the Arts, the New York State Council on the Arts, and the New York City Department of Cultural Affairs.

T&W also thanks the following foundations and corporations: American Stock Exchange, Anonymous Donor, Apple Computer Inc., Bertelsmann USA, The Bingham Trust, Bronx City Council, The Bydale Foundation, Chase Manhattan Bank, Consolidated Edison, Simon and Eve Colin Foundation, Charles E. Culpeper Foundation, Farrar, Straus and Giroux, Heckscher Foundation for Children, Morgan Stanley Foundation, M&O Foundation, NYNEX Foundation, Prudential Foundation, Queens City Council, Maurice R. Robinson Fund, Helena Rubinstein Foundation, and the Scherman Foundation.

Teachers & Writers Collaborative
5 Union Square West
New York, N.Y. 10003-3306

Cover and page design: Christopher Edgar
Printed by Philmark Lithographics, New York, N.Y.

Permissions

Table of Contents

xi Preface / *Julio Marzán*

1 Missing the Zebras: Bilingual Poetry in the Schools / *Julia Alvarez*

22 Ode to Pablo Neruda : Using Neruda's Odes in the Creative Writing Classroom / *Martín Espada*

33 Writing Poems Inspired by Lorca / *Kenneth Koch*

47 Lorca for High School and College Students / *Kenneth Koch and Kate Farrell*

54 Waiting, Listening, and Wondering: Using Three Poems by Mayra Jiménez, Homero Aridjis, and Ernesto Cardenal / *Mark Statman*

66 To You/For You, Para Ti: Using a Poem by Miguel Hernández / *Janine Pommy Vega*

79 Inspiring Young Writers with Chicano *Pinto* Poetry / *Mary Sue Galindo*

87 Questions We Didn't Know We Wanted to Ask: Using Neruda / *Deborah Cummins*

94 Talking to Lorca's Moon / *Rosemarie Roqué*

101 Writing Vignettes with Sandra Cisneros's *House on Mango Street* / *Suzann Steele Saltzman*

109 The Flowered Song: Learning from Aztec and Mexican Poetry / *John Oliver Simon*

121 Singing with the Words: Using Pablo Neruda and Federico García Lorca with Middle School Students / *Carol Bearse*

146 Sound, Rhythm, Music: Using a Poem by Nicolás Guillén / *William Bryant Logan*

151   Ritmo y vida / Rhythm and Life: A Voyage with Lorca / *David Mills*

157   Antonio Machado's "Childhood Memory" / *David Unger*

163   A Moment of Change: Using a Poem by Juan Ramón Jiménez / *Janine Pommy Vega*

169   Introducing the *Greguería*—and Ramón Gómez de la Serna / *Bill Zavatsky*

183   Día de dulce / Sweet Day: Using Paz, Pacheco, Gutiérrez, Deltoro, and Blanco / *Naomi Shihab Nye*

193   Reading and Seeing: Teaching Bilingual Calligrams / *Mark Statman*

204   Other Models / *Ron Padgett and Julio Marzán*

223   Bibliography and Other Resources

228   Notes on Contributors

Preface

by Julio Marzán

Early in his career, William Carlos Williams received a letter that challenged his American pedigree, calling him a "bloomin' foreigner" whose ancestral involvement with the country didn't extend much beyond the East Coast and whose mind was muddied up by Spanish. The letter was from his friend Ezra Pound, whose remarks always provoked Williams to exhibit even more confidently the American consciousness that is the hallmark of his work. Williams believed his work was enriched by his bicultural heritage, from his Anglo father and his Puerto Rican mother, whose Spanish forebears had planted their roots in the length and breadth of America a century before Jamestown. In fact, it was partly Williams' determination to infuse into American English elements of his mother's tongue, to establish his own spiritual and poetic "line," that led to his revolutionizing the contemporary American aesthetic.

Around the middle of this century, this aesthetic began receiving another strong infusion of Hispanic culture, as the country belatedly discovered the poetry of Lorca and subsequently Neruda (two poets whom Williams perceived as spiritual brothers descending from a common "line"), as well as Vallejo, and, more recently, fiction writers such as Borges and García Márquez—a flowering of great writing that has had an international impact. Canadian Tom Wayman has described how, in writing a poem, he once actually felt the presence of Neruda in the room. The number of American poets who have written tributes to Vallejo could fill a volume of poetry. Since the 1970s, how much American fiction descends from writers who were ultimately students of Borges, who himself wouldn't have been Borges (a.k.a. Pierre Menard) were it not for Cervantes?

Unfortunately, these cultural contributions are rarely acknowledged as such: credit is given to individual writers, but it is as if, in the Anglo's perception, these geniuses actually stood apart from the Latin world. Such an attitude notwithstanding, the contributions of Williams, Lorca, and numerous other Latin American writers are incontrovertible; also contrary to popular assumptions, today's nascent Latino writing does not materialize rootless. Thus, teachers of writing who use Hispanic models are filling a significant gap in all students' literary consciousness, not just those who are Latino. When it comes to literature, all Americans have a multicultural national heritage.

Many teachers feel the need to use Hispanic writing because they have Hispanic students, who will naturally respond to it with more than usual interest. But it should be underscored that the ethnic focus of this book is secondary. The teachers and writers who share their experiences in this book not only display respect for the literary nature of the texts they write about, but also enthusiasm, itself a valuable teaching aid. In all cases, the intention is to introduce all students to models that they can emulate in their own imaginative writing.

Consequently, I have selected essays that offer an appreciation of the literary work as well as advice in teaching specific writing techniques. Bill Zavatsky introduces his translations of de la Serna's *greguerías* to us as well as his students, who produce some extraordinarily worthy imitations of these one-line poems. Martín Espada's use of Neruda's odes not only asks students to address objects but to imagine the unimportant in epic dimensions. Mark Statman helps us to enjoy the visual poem through an acknowledged master of the genre, the Mexican Juan José Tablada. In a second essay, Statman demonstrates how three poems, one each by Mayra Jiménez, Homero Aridjis, and Ernesto Cardenal, remind us of the importance of being tuned into our senses. Julia Alvarez encourages her bilingual students to explore the richness of seeing the world in parallel languages. Similarly, Kenneth Koch asks students to insert words from Spanish to evoke a nuance different from that of the corresponding English words. In a different essay, Koch and Kate Farrell take us directly into the mysteriousness of Lorca's poetry. Mary Sue Galindo shows tough students that poets and writing are even found among Chicano prisoners. Rosemarie Roqué asks her students to talk to the magical figure Luna, as the boy talks to her in Lorca's famous poem. Janine Pommy Vega uses Juan Ramón Jiménez to explore a moment of change, after which nothing is the same. In a second essay, she asks students to express their feelings toward someone, as Miguel Hernández did in writing to his son from the Spanish Civil War. Deborah Cummins has students write poems consisting entirely of questions, questions we didn't know were important until we read them in a poem, in the manner of Neruda's *Book of Questions*. Suzann Steele Saltzman teaches her students to write vignettes about where they live, after Sandra Cisneros's life on Mango Street. Carol Bearse uses Neruda to teach students the art of naming things with metaphors. William Bryant Logan has students write poems that use rhythm and sound as music as Nicolás Guillén did in "Sensemayá." David Mills asks his students to imagine—like Lorca, who was traveling to Santiago, Cuba—that they will be going somewhere and to write a chant that describes the things that will be different when they get there, adding rhythm to evoke the joy of arriving. After reading her students several Mexican poems (by Paz, Pacheco, Blanco, and Gutiérrez), Naomi Shihab Nye takes her students for a walk around their changing San Antonio neighborhood, to gather images for poems on things they never paid attention to before, things that are more valuable to them than they had thought. David Unger reads Antonio Machado's "Childhood Memory" of a stiff teacher and dim classroom, asking students to observe how the poet's feeling toward that memory is expressed in the tone and subtlety of the poem's detailed imagery. John Oliver Simon introduces his students to the notion of the "flowered word," through which the Aztecs talked to their gods.

Clearly, some poets are writing class stars: Neruda and Lorca top the list. While several of the contributors to this volume use these two poets, the essays highlight different poems and propose distinct literary challenges. We also include a wide variety of other styles and writers, perhaps less well known but no less useful. An additional resource is an appendix of even more writing models, for although this book is not intended to be a representative anthology of contemporary Latin American, Spanish, and Latino writing, we did want to suggest the range of these literatures. For those teachers interested in giving their students even more poems, there is a bibliography of books used by the essay authors, as well as a few that I have added.

JULIA ALVAREZ

Missing the Zebras
Bilingual Poetry in the Schools

I used to sing a bilingual song as a child in Santo Domingo:

Pollito: chicken,
Gallina: hen,
Lápiz: pencil,
Pluma: pen.

The song was obviously mechanical (like singing your multiplication tables), but I couldn't get enough of it. What delighted me most was the idea that I had two names for the same thing. It's difficult to explain the excitement of this to someone who has not grown up in two languages—I suppose you could compare it to that small surprise of seeing twins.

In a bilingual Poetry-in-the-School program in an elementary school in Wilmington, Delaware, some years ago, I tried to convey to the children this same sense of linguistic wealth that comes from knowing both Spanish and English. Too often in these bilingual programs or programs for "special groups," we tend to focus on what is underprivileged in the kids, what has been left out, what they do not have that they must get: we must bring them up to grade level; we must make them confident and dominant in one language; or, *Ay Dios*, we must make them proud of who they are. Such a philosophy assumes that they aren't already proud, or if they aren't, confirms their insecurities. I am not minimizing the very real difficulties, gaps, and insecurities these children have experienced. But why always approach them at the sorest, bleakest place in their experience? My goal during a four-week residency at Mary C. I. Williams Elementary School was to explore—as a Dominican-American myself, with the kids in the classroom—what special insights into language, rhythm, imagination, and experience we had as products of two cultures. And, of course, we had to have fun!

But how to approach these goals? Would I merely do a translation of the poetry program as I had given it in English: Kenneth Koch à la San

1

Juan? I tried that in my first, combined fourth–fifth grade bilingual class. Speaking in Spanish and shifting (as the students themselves did) into English whenever they didn't understand something in one language or the other, I asked them what they wished for. Silence. I read them wish poems by kids in English. (I translated as I went along for the benefit of those who were Spanish-dominant.) My students laughed and poked fun at the wishes: I wish the sky was a great big bathtub....

"Ah, man," one of the kids broke out, "that's stupid!"

Obviously, these poems were not ringing true to *these* inner-city kids. "Well," I countered, "what do you wish for?"

He piped right up. "I wish I were in Puerto Rico!" The whole class clapped and yelled, "Sí, sí!"

After two years of working in poetry programs, I was cagey enough to know I could turn this outbreak to poetry by asking them to wish for things that were in Puerto Rico. I knew the class of mostly Puerto Rican children had responded so vehemently to what the student said because there was a homesickness, a nostalgia that I could remember feeling for years when I first came to this country. Wishing for what was missing was paralyzing—so much was lost—but writing about these losses might bring the lost objects back, especially if these were described in precise, fresh details. So we started a game I christened "Aquí no hay . . . pero aquí sí hay" (Here there isn't . . . but there is), which turned into a vengeful and gleeful listing of grievances: no *mangos, yuccas, merengues, Reyes Magos.* The American "replacements" were bleak:

Aquí no hay mangos como soles
pero sí hay frutas plásticas
y zafacones.

There are no mangos here like suns
but plastic fruit
and trash cans.

I pointed out that there were mangos in the supermarkets, and my students defended their choice by saying that mangos from supermarkets weren't the same as mangos from *mercados.* I asked why, and for a while they gave me the easy answer that will never do for poetry: they just *are* different. Then, little Wanda thought out the reason I'll give in translation: "In Puerto Rico, the mangos look grown." This was poetry, *epa!*

We spent the next half hour sitting in a circle on the floor talking about what we missed about our native countries. Then—these incredible "teaching aids"!—it started to snow and the kids raced to the window to watch. It struck me that we had been concentrating on the losses and replacements, but had not mentioned the startling new things we had never encountered before: snow, for one! I made my own comparison: before, we had eaten *frío-frío (literally* "cold-cold," snow cones), but now we could eat *la nieve fría* (cold snow). They smiled knowingly. I then asked them to tell me all the things they had first seen in this country. I could hardly hear their answers—there were so many discoveries to tell about that they kept interrupting each other.

My goal here in describing a class in action was to concentrate on the unique vision of a bilingual, bicultural child. One of the insights I gained can be seen in the exercise described above: these children have a wealth of images and experiences from—not one—but two cultures. Because they have lived in two cultures and two languages, they have that uncanny insight of the rootless. One of the writing ideas they enjoyed came to me through Whitman—that wanderer who wrote down the sights and smells and sounds of America. I pointed out to the children that they too were "experts," had traveled, and seen a lot more than most children their age. In combination with Whitman, I read them García Lorca's "Ode to Walt Whitman" in Spanish from *Poet in New York*. Then I had them become "gypsy poets" and jot down interesting, sad, tiny events, people, sounds, and smells that had captivated them in their transit between cultures and countries.

The advantage of working with a bilingual group is that poems from both languages can be used in the original—Whitman in English, García Lorca in Spanish. Of course, the Spanish-dominant students had problems with the English poems and vice versa. So I always supplied a translation or, with their help, translated the poem on the board. The students enjoyed these on-the-spot translations—like a class collaboration without the pressure to think up something and with the pleasure of "getting two poems out of one," the old loaves and fishes miracle!

These translation exercises and the excitement they created gave me the idea of a charades game that could later be turned into a writing exercise. On pieces of paper, I copied down words the students gave me, the English word on one side, its Spanish equivalent on the other. After filling a bag with wonderful and zany words, we each picked a slip and silently acted out the word. The challenge was to guess the word in both languages. This led to a discussion of how words changed from one language to another—how at first it had been so strange to say cup instead of *vaso*, house and not *casa*. We then wrote poems about that first encounter with a new word in a new language: What did you think when you first heard *star*? Did you have any inkling it was an *estrella*? What did you see, smell, hear in the new sound? One of my English-dominant students wrote about his encounter with the word *ola* ("wave," as in the ocean):

> If I didn't know
> what an *ola* was,
> I'd think it was a star.
> I'd think it was smoke
> in the house
> or a heavy blue coat
> to go out.
>
> —*Raul Rivera, second grade*

From this exercise, we moved on to Nicolás Guillén's *Great Zoo* poems, in which Guillén cages abstract words. In the following poem, translated by Robert Márquez, we meet Hunger:

El hambre

Esta es el hambre. Un animal
todo colmillo y ojo.
Nadie le engaña ni distrae.
No se harta en una mesa.
No se contenta
con un almuerzo o una cena.
Anuncia siempre sangre.
Ruge como león, aprieta como boa,
piensa como persona.

El ejemplar que aquí se ofrece
fue cazado en la India (*suburbios de Bombay*),
pero existe en estado más o menos salvaje
en otras muchas partes.

No acercarse.

Hunger

This is hunger. An animal
all fangs and eyes.
It cannot be distracted or deceived.
It is not satisfied with one meal.

It is not content
with a lunch or a dinner.
Always threatens blood.
Roars like a lion, squeezes like a boa,
thinks like a person.

The specimen before you
was captured in India (*outskirts of Bombay*),
but it exists in a more or less savage state
in many other places.

Please stand back.

Inspired by Guillén, my students each caged a word in either language
and described the concrete beast behind bars:

Shyness/Vergüenza

She sits back in far
corners of the cage
with a turtleneck
pulled up over
her face.

  —Anonymous

Vanity/Vanidad

All alone, too good for anyone.
Sticking her nose in the air
as all pass by.
Primping and primping half of
the day.
Greedy for everything, everything
has to be hers.
But still too good for anyone.

  —T.C., sixth grade

Not only do these students have two cultures and two languages to
make poems out of, they can also bring these together in interesting combinations. Many contrast poems came out of describing an experience in
one country and language and the same experience in the new country and
language: *Navidad* in Puerto Rico versus Christmas in Delaware; something that happened *en la escuela* versus in school; having your hair cut in
either country. For those who didn't want to use two languages or "couldn't

remember" anything from Puerto Rico, I asked them to write in one language something they had seen or smelled or touched at home that was different from a similar experience in a supermarket, a doctor's office, or an Anglo friend's home.

In general, I tried as often as possible to use Spanish-language poets and give the children a sense of the incredible literary wealth of their native cultures. They felt so excited to discover that very famous poets had come from their own countries. Neruda's odes (especially "Ode to My Socks," "Ode to the Scissors," "Ode to the Watermelon," and "Ode to My Clothes") were immediate favorites and led to a writing exercise in which students chose a very simple object—an orange, a girl's lips—and wrote an ode celebrating that object. A way to make this exercise a lesson in both cultures is to have students bring to class an object that they identify with their native culture and then write an ode to that object. A Latina student might bring in her black onyx, good-luck *azabache* or an Aguila baseball cap or a *colador* for making coffee. An Anglo student might bring in a Red Sox baseball cap or an eggbeater or a television remote-control device.

Whatever the lesson plan or poem, I found that my students were eager to express themselves on issues that so deeply affected them. This was especially so because they could use their native language at least as a starting point. In this multicultural and multilingual environment, they began to feel more at home in their adopted country and, most importantly, in *el gran zoo* of their imaginations, as in this poem by sixth grader José Rodríguez:

El prisionero

Estuve 99 años
en una jaula
por matar un perro.
Y le alcé la voz
a los polícias.
Por poco me colgaron.
Desde ese tiempo
me acostumbré a ver
barrillas negras.
Mañana cuando salga
me van a hacer falta
esas cebras que me tenían
preso.

The Prisoner

For ninety-nine years
I've lived behind bars
for killing a dog.
I raised my voice
at the cops.
They almost hanged me.
Since that time
I got used
to black stripes.
Tomorrow when they set me free
I'm going to miss
the zebras that imprisoned me.

ANTHOLOGY

Inspired by Nicolás Guillén's Great Zoo

Los celos

Los celos son mellizos.
Una tiene una muñeca
y la otra no tiene nada.
Una tiene celos
y la otra no.

Jealousies

Jealousies are identical twins.
One has a doll
the other has nothing.
One is jealous
and the other one no.

—*Daisy Rodríguez, third grade*

La soledad

La Soledad
es
una flor
que

crece por todo el mundo
y
nadie
la ve.

Solitude

Solitude
is
a flower
that grows all over the world
and
nobody
sees it.

　　　—*Lissette, fifth grade*

El amor

El Amor
es
un niño colorado.

Love

Love
is
a red boy.

　　　—*José M., first grade*

El silencio

El Silencio
es
una arañita
tejiendo
alas.
Cuando
termina,
sube
a
las nubes.

Silence

Silence
is
a little spider
knitting
wings.
When
she's done,
she climbs up
to
the clouds.

—Angel, second grade

La muerte

La muerte es un camión
cargado de silencio
que va al hospital.
El doctor lo está guiando.

Death

Death is a truck
loaded with silence
going to the hospital.
The doctor is driving.

—Javier, second grade

Inspired by Neruda's Odes

Oda a los labios

Labios,
tú pareces una máquina de besos.
Los enamorados te usan mucho . . .
y las madres y los padres también
cuando los hijos se van de su lado.

Me ayudas a hablar
a leer
a rezar.

9

Julia Alvarez

Labios,
por fin
encontrastes otros labios
en la cara
de una muchacha.

Ode to Lips

Lips, you're a kissing machine.
Lovers use you a lot...
and mothers and fathers as well
when their children leave their side.

You help me to talk
to read
to pray.

Lips,
at last
you've found other lips
on the face
of a girl.

—*José Rodríguez, sixth grade*

Oda a la naranja

Naranja,
tú pareces una sortija de oro,
pero a tí te comemos
hasta que no queda nada
menos la cáscara y las semillas.

Pero de esas semillas
salen tus hijos,
crecen como tú
pero también nos los comemos.

Naranja,
no te vale tener hijos
si van a morir
en mi boca.

Ode to the Orange

Orange,
you look like a gold ring,
but we eat you up
until there's nothing left
but skin and seeds.

Your sons grow
from those seeds,
they look like you
and we eat them too.

Orange,
it's not worth your having kids
if they're going to die
in my mouth.

> —*Lissette Rivera, Sonia Roman,*
> *and José Rodríguez, fifth and sixth grades*

Inspired by Two Poems by Gabriela Mistral

La medianoche

Fina, la medianoche.
Oigo los nudos del rosal:
la savia empuja subiendo a la rosa.

Oigo
las rayas quemadas del tigre
real: no le dejan dormir.

Oigo
la estrofa de uno,
y le crece en la noche
como la duna.

Oigo
a mi madre dormida
con dos alientos.
(Duermo yo en ella,
de cincos años.)

Oigo el Ródano
que baja y que me lleva como un padre
ciego de espuma ciega.

Y después nada oigo
sino que voy cayendo
en los muros
llenos de sol . . .

      —Gabriela Mistral

Midnight

Delicate, the midnight.
I hear the nodes of the rosebush:
the sap pushes up the tree.

I hear
the burnt stripes of the royal tiger:
they don't let him sleep.

I hear
the poem of someone,
it grows in the night
like a dune.

I hear
my mother sleeping,
breathing two breaths.
(In her I sleep,
five years old.)

I hear the Rhone's rush
that falls and carries me like a father
blind with blind foam.

And then I hear nothing,
but I am falling
on walls
full of sunlight.

      —Translated by Doris Dana

Sonidos

Estoy en mi cama.
Oigo
a mi mamá bajando
por las escaleras.

Oigo
un carro guiando solo.

Oigo
una mujer caminando por la acera.
Ella está hablando con las piedras,
diciéndole que se acuesten.

Es tarde.

Oigo un gato
que llora con hambre.

Oigo
el corazón haciendo ruido
como si alguien me estuviera
dando en el pecho.

Sounds

I'm in bed.
I hear
my mother going
downstairs.

I hear
a car driving itself.

I hear
a woman walking on the sidewalk.
She's talking to the stones,
telling them to sleep.

It's late.

I hear a cat
crying with hunger.

I hear
my heart make noises

as if someone were
knocking on my chest.

—Rafael López, third grade

Cosas
(*extractos*)

1.
Amo las cosas que nunca tuve
con las otras que ya no tengo:

Yo toco un agua silenciosa,
parada en pastos friolentos,
que sin un viento tiritaba
en el huerto que era mi huerto.

La miro como la miraba;
me da un extraño pensamiento,
y juego, lenta, con esa agua
como con pez o con misterio.

2.
Pienso en umbral donde dejé
pasos alegres que ya no llevo,
y en el umbral veo una llaga
llena de musgo y de silencio.

3.
Me busco un verso que he perdido,
que a los siete años me dijeron.
Fue una mujer haciendo el pan
y yo su santa boca veo.

4.
Viene un aroma roto en ráfagas;
soy muy dichosa si lo siento;
de tan delgado no es aroma,
siendo el olor de los almendros.

5.
Me vuelve niños los sentidos;
le busco un nombre y no lo acierto,
y huelo el aire y los lugares
buscando almendros que no encuentro . . .

6.
Un río suena siempre cerca.
Ha cuarenta años que lo siento.
Es canturía de mi sangre
o bien un ritmo que me dieron.

[. . .]

9.
Amo una piedra de Oaxaca
o Guatemala, a que me acerco,
roja y fija como mi cara
y cuya grieta da un aliento.

Al dormirme queda desnuda;
no sé por qué yo la volteo,
Y tal vez nunca la he tenido
y es mi sepulcro lo que veo . . .

　　—*Gabriela Mistral*

Things
(*excerpts*)

1.
I love some things I never had
along with things I now don't have.

I touch a quiet water
caught in a cold ground
that shivered without wind
in an orchard that used to be mine.

I watch it as I used to watch it;
it gives me strange ideas,
and I play, slowly, with that water
like a fish or a mystery.

2.
I think of a threshold where I left
happy footsteps I no longer carry,
and there I see a crack
full of moss and silence.

3.
I try to find a poem I lost,
given to me when I was seven
by a woman baking bread.
I still see her saintly mouth.

4.
There's a perfume scattered by wind;
I'm lucky if I feel it;
it's so thin it's not a perfume
just the smell of the almond trees.

5.
My senses become children;
I search for the name but can't remember it.
I smell air and places
searching for trees I can't find.

6.
I hear a river close by.
I've heard it for forty years.
It's a song in my blood,
a rhythm I was given . . .

[. . .]

9.
I love a stone in Oaxaca
or Guatemala. I move towards it.
Red and firm like my face
its cracks strengthen me.

As I sleep it undresses—
I don't know why I turn it over.
Maybe I've never seen it before
and it's my grave I've discovered.

  —*Translated by Doris Dana*

What I Remember

I left Puerto Rico
when I was a year old.
I used to call my mother "Mami."
I used to go all around the house

playing with my ball.
I used to smell coffee, rich
like mountain grown.
My mother used to put me on hot sand
without shoes
and my feet got so hot
that I had to learn how to walk.

—Angel Rivera, third grade

Puerto Rico

Si volara a Puerto Rico
me iría al mar
a bañarme en el agua salada.
Si volara a Puerto Rico
me iría a los montes
a trabajar en la tierra.
Si volara a Puerto Rico
me tiraría al sol
para sacarme el frío
de mi cuerpo.

Puerto Rico

If I flew to Puerto Rico
I'd go to the sea
and bathe in salt water.
If I flew to Puerto Rico
I'd go to the woods
to work on the earth.
If I flew to Puerto Rico
I'd throw myself in the sun
to take out the cold
in my bones.

—Luis Olivera, sixth grade

Inspired by Alvaro Yunque's "Cuando sea grande"

Cuando sea grande

Mamá, cuando sea grande,

voy a hacer una escalera
tan alta que llegue al cielo,
para ir a coger estrellas.

Me llenaré los bolsillos
de estrellas y de cometas,
y bajaré a repartirlas
a los chicos de la escuela.

Pero a ti voy a traerte,
mamá, la luna llena,
para que alumbres la casa
sin gastar en luz eléctrica.

    —Alvaro Yunque

When I Grow Up

Mother, when I grow up
I'm going to build a ladder
tall enough to reach the sky
so I can go star-picking.

I'll fill my pockets
with stars and comets,
and come down to distribute them
among the kids at school.

But for you I'm bringing,
Mother, the full moon,
so you can light up the house
without spending on electricity.

    —Translated by Julia Alvarez

Cuando yo era chiquita

Mi mamá se fue al doctor
cuando yo nací.
Y despues cuando vino
a ver,
ya yo tenía un año.

Donde mi abuela
nadie me estaba velando,

yo—como no sabía nada—
me estaba comiendo la tierra.

When I Was Little

My mother went to the doctor
when I was born.
And before she
knew it,
I was one year old.

At my grandmother's
no one was watching me
and since I didn't know any better
I was eating the earth.

—*Daisy Rodríguez, third grade*

One poem inspired by a combination of Neruda and Guillén

Pez,
tú estas en el agua,
Pez.
Nadando,
Pez,
en el agua.

Soy yo,
Pez.
Juega,
Pez,
en el agua.

Soy yo, Pez, una mariposa.

Fish,
you are in the water,
Fish.
Swimming,
Fish,
in the water

It's me,
Fish.

Play,
Fish,
in the water.

It's me, Fish, a butterfly.

  —*Julio Rosam, second grade*

Inspired by Lorca's "La luna asoma"

La luna asoma

Cuando sale la luna
se pierden las campanas
y aparecen las sendas
impenetrables.

Cuando sale la luna,
el mar cubre la tierra
y el corazón se siente
isla en el infinito.

Nadie come naranjas
bajo la luna llena.
Es preciso comer
fruta verde y helada.

Cuando sale la luna
de cien rostros iguales,
la moneda de plata
solloza en el bolsillo.

  —*Federico García Lorca*

The Moon Rising

When the moon rises,
the bells hang silent,
and impenetrable footpaths
appear.

When the moon rises,
the sea covers the land,
and the heart feels
like an island in infinity.

Nobody eats oranges
under the full moon.
One must eat fruit
that is green and cold.

When the moon rises,
moon of a hundred equal faces,
the silver coin
sobs in the pocket.

—Translated by Lysander Kemp

Cuando el viento

Cuando el viento sopla
los arboles bailan.

Cuando el viento sopla
mi corazón me late.

Cuando el viento sopla
los pajaritos se vuelven papeles,
bailan,
y lo siente el viento de mi alma.

When the Wind

When the wind blows
the trees dance.

When the wind blows
my heart beats.

When the wind blows
the birds turn into papers,
they dance,
and the wind in my soul knows it.

—Angel Manuel, fifth grade

[*Note: All the translations of children's poems in this essay are by Julia Alvarez.*]

MARTÍN ESPADA

Ode to Pablo Neruda

Using Neruda's Odes in the Creative Writing Classroom

Let me begin with a confession. The fact that I am teaching at all amazes me. True, I am guilty of committing poetry. And it is equally true that those who conspire to commit poetry often teach. I even bear the title of "Associate Professor," a credential that conceals my origins. I failed English once, in the eighth grade. I was the sullen youth lurking in the high school parking lot, far more concerned with the amateur exploration of pharmaceuticals than with the lyrics of light opera I was once forced to read aloud in class by a grim-faced English teacher. More damaging still . . . I became a lawyer.

My personal journey from the high school parking lot to the courtroom to the classroom is the stuff of some other essay. My point here is that, as a teacher, I am always asking myself these questions: How would I teach that younger version of myself? How can I reach the student who may well evolve into a poet, given that a poetic sensibility may be brewing in even the most marginalized and alienated of students? How can I, with a literary and educational background that my colleagues charitably describe as "unorthodox," channel the glowing energy of a creative writing classroom? Conveniently, all these questions have the same answer: Pablo Neruda.

The Chilean Nobel Prize winner is considered by many to be the greatest Latin American poet of the twentieth century. Gabriel García Márquez maintains that Neruda was the greatest poet of this century in *any* language. There are many Nerudas: the love poet, the surrealist, the political poet, the creator of historical epics, the poet of the sea. For our purposes, he is the poet who revolutionized an ancient form: the ode. His odes— with their clarity and depth, their simple diction and complex emotion, their playful humor, their insistence on the senses and the image, their use of hyperbole, their celebration of existence—are ideal vehicles to inspire the creation of poetry in the classroom.

22

The ode is, indeed, an ancient form. By definition, this is a poem of praise and celebration, originally meant to be sung in public. The classical poets Pindar and Horace were renowned for their odes. Those who remember the ode from high school were probably introduced to Percy Bysshe Shelley's "Ode to the West Wind." Over the centuries, the ode became a form laden with classical references and great themes, its tone lofty and solemn.

Neruda wrote odes in everyday language about everyday things and people. By writing an ode to the "ordinary," the poet demanded dignity for the commonplace subject, commanding respect for things and people normally denied such respect. There is an appreciation here for a wide array of subjects: socks, a suit, salt, the atom, watermelon, scissors, French fries, a tuna in the market, the village movie theater, a dead carob tree, a stamp album, a ship in a bottle, the dictionary, a laboratory technician, a gentle bricklayer. There are odes that sprang from immediate experience: the poet once fell down, landed on his head, then wrote an ode to his cranium. There are anti-odes as well: a sardonic ode to literary criticism, for example. Taken together, the odes express a sense of wonder at being alive, an all-embracing passion for existence. In the words of the critic René de Costa, for Neruda, "*nothing* is gratuitous."

De Costa notes that Neruda's odes employ various strategies. The poem will often begin with a metaphor that establishes the poetic dignity of the subject, defining the subject as worthy of odic treatment. Neruda often concluded his odes with a moral, a philosophical note. Rather than dwell on the lessons his readers should learn, however, Neruda emphasized what *he* had learned from his experience with the thing or person celebrated in the poem. The didactic function of the poems was apparent to the poet, and indeed Neruda's work exemplified the idea that an ode should not only relish existence, but teach others to do the same.

In the process, Neruda perfected the art of hyperbole, a device very well suited to the ode. Deliberate exaggeration, which nonetheless states the truth of the matter, lends itself nicely to a poetic form dedicated to praise and celebration. In Neruda's odes we can observe the poet engaging in the hyperbolic exploration of all five senses. So it is that a tiny organism beneath the lens of a microscope becomes a dragon, or an infection under that lens becomes "a black nimbus."

The epic political poet of *Canto general* surprised everyone when his odes began to emerge in the mid-1950s. According to de Costa, Neruda began writing the odes at the request of his friend, Miguel Otero Silva, to be published in Otero Silva's newspaper, *El Nacional,* in Caracas. This accounts for their shape on the page, a narrow column designed to fit in a newspaper. The first ode appeared in *El Nacional* on October 16, 1952, but most of the odes appeared in four books published between 1954 and 1959: *Odas elementales* (*Elemental Odes*); *Nuevas odas elementales* (*New Elemental Odes*); *Tercer libro de las odas* (*Third Book of Odes*); and *Navagaciones y regresos* (*Voyages and Homecomings*). The odes are also widely available in translation. (I recommend *Selected Odes of Pablo Neruda,* translated by Margaret Sayers Peden, whose versions I quote from in this essay, unless otherwise noted.)

These odes were so accessible that even an audience lacking a formal education could understand them. With the odes, Neruda, for years an advocate for the "common" people, became a poet *of* the people: the bricklayer not only as subject, but as audience. As de Costa tells it, Neruda was now "a citizen poet...an artistic utility." His poetry was now "a useful public service." This egalitarian approach to his audience was a natural outgrowth of his radical politics, a logical next step after his *Canto general.*

Neruda wanted his odes to be useful: "I want people to enter a hardware / store through the door of my odes." I have most often worked with three of Neruda's odes in the classroom, namely "Ode to My Socks," "Ode to Salt," and "Ode to the Watermelon," though dozens of the other odes could serve the same purpose. I have used these most useful of poems to stimulate writing by middle and high school students, high school teachers, college undergraduates, and prison inmates. The poems serve both as illustrations of certain poetic principles and as models for student writing.

Anyone who teaches Neruda's odes should, first of all, read as many as possible beforehand. The variety of his odes is so enormous that a teacher may well discover a poem that perfectly reflects the students' environment or curiosities. But the odes are useful for more than a discussion of their subject matter. They also demonstrate the literary devices that construct the ode. If the ode is a house—and, indeed, Neruda wrote a poem called "The House of Odes"—then the tools to build that house include metaphor, simile, hyperbole, personification, oxymoron, and irony, among others in the crowded toolbox.

Often I begin by having one student read the poem aloud in English and another read it in Spanish. Even those students who do not speak Neruda's language can appreciate the music of the words—the tangible presence of his voice—and those who do speak Spanish are empowered by the attention devoted to their language. Suddenly and dramatically, these students become the experts. I always work from a bilingual text, and give students the choice of writing in either language, using either the original or translation of the poem as a road map to begin the journey into their own poetry.

Before using the poem as a model for writing, however, the students must have a solid grasp of the poem as ode, and the construction of its machinery. After we read the poem, I define my terms, whether ode, metaphor, simile, or hyperbole. However, I never try to introduce all these concepts *for the first time* during the same class. This would be too much to absorb and instantly apply to the creation of a poem in class, adding confusion to the agreeable chaos that prevails in my classroom. For example, though metaphor and simile are easily taught from the ode, I introduce them in an earlier class, then remind students that what they learned previously about building an image should be applied to writing an ode.

The element that I most often discuss is hyperbole. Students gravitate towards that concept intuitively. They use hyperbole in everyday speech without realizing it. Once younger students comprehend that hyperbole includes a phrase like "when the cat threw up on the shag carpet, I could have died," then demystification takes place, and hyperbolic verbiage sprouts all over the classroom. Everyone loves to exaggerate (which is itself an exaggeration, but then I am a hyperbolist). The ode/hyperbole combination gives students license to explore a range of emotions.

The next step, after reading the poem and defining poetic devices, is to search the poem for examples of these devices in action. Alerted to Neruda's strategy of dignifying the "ordinary" subject, the students identify the dignifying metaphor(s) in the poem. In "Ode to Salt," for instance, Neruda begins by telling us that the salt "sings" in the salt mines, "with a mouth smothered / by the earth," "a / broken/ voice, / a mournful / song." The first stanza will usually yield a key dignifying metaphor. In the opening stanza of "Ode to My Socks," Neruda refers to these underappreciated articles of clothing as "jewel cases," and in the next stanza characterizes those same socks as "woven fire."

Of course, the phrases "jewel cases" and "woven fire" are also prime examples of hyperbole. If the students are advanced, I point out the distinction between metaphor and hyperbole. Some metaphors are not hyperbolic; not every hyperbole is metaphorical.

We then move on to identifying the multiple uses of hyperbole in the ode. The "Ode to the Watermelon" is studded with examples. In the Robert Bly translation, we see watermelon as the "coolest of all the planets," the "green whale of summer," a "jewel box of water," the "queen of the fruitshops," a "moon on earth," a "mountain or a mine," "rubies," "star-filled," dissolving into "wild rivers," and so on. Here we witness Neruda's attention to sensory detail—to color, texture, taste, shape, and size—as he builds his hyperbolic images. Tools, such as hyperbole, are themselves constructed objects.

Since Neruda's odes frequently have an educational purpose, the class debates the larger questions raised by the poem. "Ode to Salt" raises such questions: Where does salt come from? Who are the salt miners? What is the connection between salt and suffering? How are we implicated in the suffering of the salt? Do we take salt, and the labors of salt, for granted? If the salt in the saltshaker could be born of suffering, what does that say about the everyday objects all around us?

I divide class time into thirds. Exploration of the poem occupies approximately the first third of the session. Following that exploration, the students receive an assignment: simply, to write an ode, a poem in praise of something or someone great or small, ordinary or extraordinary. The mission is to educate us about the subject, but also to persuade the reader or listener of the subject's importance. Students should consciously use hyperbole to construct the ode, and remember to use metaphor and simile as devices for constructing hyperbole. Students then write in class.

In general, the more advanced the students, the more time allotted for in-class writing. An eighth grader will probably exhaust his or her resources after fifteen to twenty minutes of working on a ode; an adult, however, will need a minimum of an hour, drafting the poem two or three times. Younger students will more likely be comfortable with the structure of working at a desk in a classroom, whereas more mature students appreciate the opportunity to disperse, choosing a spot to sit and write in the vicinity of the classroom. I circulate during writing time, consulting with students and attending to the occasional case of writer's block. This can be a challenge when the students have scattered. Once I found a student riding up and down in an elevator, squatting on the floor and scribbling wildly. Writing occupies approximately the middle third of class time.

During the final third of class time, I have students read their work aloud, not for critical response—that comes from me later, in writing, when poems are handed in—but to build solidarity among students based on the sense of discovery that comes with hearing one another's attempts to create the same kind of poem. I ask students to listen for images and hyperbole they find striking; this is not only an exercise in writing, and reading aloud, but an attempt to cultivate the skill of listening as well, a skill so necessary to the creation of poetry. After each poem, I elicit brief responses: What did you hear? What images linger in the mind, like ghosts?

The students' odes are usually as diverse and surprising as Neruda's. Some students produce solemn classical odes in praise of some imposing natural phenomenon. Others see the ode as a form of expression for honoring humanity, and produce a poem in praise of an unknown, unsung individual. Still others celebrate personal identity. Many praise the small creatures all around us. Then there are those, at all levels, who use the ode as an opportunity to become utterly goofy. The anti-ode turns up on occasion. And a few boldly accept this additional challenge from me: to write an ode in praise of something I despise, like the walnut, and convince me of its greatness, for the writer of the ode must finally be convincing.

The student odes from my classes and workshops provide the best illustration of this thematic diversity. Most of the odes my students have written are lost to me, but I have salvaged a few. Many reflect Neruda's influence, and some of them echo Neruda's subject matter or language even when the student has not seen the particular Neruda ode that resonates in his or her own poem.

Odes to nature abound. For example, Alison Stine, a high school student from Mansfield, Ohio, wrote:

Wind

I know when she is coming
for the garden trembles
with her step,
and the trees quiver as
an invisible hand
strokes their bearded heads,
and the silk bushes shudder
like a thousand butterflies
beating their ripe, green wings.

The last image is reminiscent of Neruda's "Some Beasts" about South America before the arrival of human beings, with the monkeys "startling the butterflies of Muzo / into flying violets" (Bly's translation), a poem the student had not seen.

If Neruda's language influences the student poet who writes about nature, so too does his attitude. The Nerudian ode is a lesson in appreciation, and students learn to appreciate their own landscape, as well as the people in it. Emily Glenn, a high school student from rural Delaware, Ohio, wrote a poem that was actually an ode to those in her community who *work* the land:

Ode to the Land

Silver dollar blades make the first cuts.
Criss-cross, and the land rouses,
Evening comes, and the sun sets
over an expanse of carob chunks.
Seeds, land's fertile embryos
are dropped from plastic nurseries
into cuts that do not bleed
but run rivers of welcoming mud.

This poem echoes Neruda's "Ode to Salt," with its images of the salt mines and the labors of salt.

The unsung hero is a recurring subject. For many, like Neruda (or John Lennon, for that matter), the unsung hero is a working-class hero, to whom homage is due. Neruda's "Ode to the Gentle Bricklayer" comes to mind when I read the following poem by Leif Riddington, who wrote this while an undergraduate at the University of Massachusetts-Amherst. If the subject is Nerudian, so, too, is the insistence on vivid image, metaphor, and simile. I quote this moving poem in its entirety:

To the Shipyard Welder on Vancouver Island

for my father

When I think of your hands
spraying green fire
from the welder's rocket
against the buttoned hulk of a tanker,
nursing metal with a bottle of flame,

I see the concrete tidebreaker
where I once stood twenty years ago,
tossing cement bombs at crabs
until you punched out;
my own hands
already a cradle for stone
lullabies that floated down
among the crabs
and rusty gardens of kelp;

and so I have your hard hands
and think of them swinging
a lunch pail at seagulls in the morning,
your diabetic legs, your callused lap
pricked dull with insulin,
and I wonder if, perhaps, your legs
will collapse like pecked wood
under the acres of sheet metal
they haul
before I see you again.

Neruda celebrated his identity as a poet in "The Invisible Man," an ode that can inspire middle school and high school students to write about their own identities. One middle school student in Cambridge, Massachusetts, Jethro Curry, wrote an "Ode to My Afro," with the jubilant refrain: "Praise the Afro!" Another student, whom history records only as "Nick," from Dover, Massachusetts, wrote an "Ode to My Height:"

I am a short person.
I'd like to be tall, but then
I wouldn't be short
so scratch that . . .
Although I cannot reach the sky,
I can reach the center of the earth.

Aside from the clever hyperbolic flourish of the last phrase, here is evidence that Nick has absorbed another of Neruda's lessons: to dignify through the ode that which our culture dismisses as humble.

This deep appreciation for the most humble, supposedly insignificant beings of the earth expresses itself in such Neruda odes as his "Ode to Bees" and "Ode to the Lizard." An Ohio high school teacher in a writing workshop, Rebekah Burkholder, wrote "Ode to the Ant," with an admirable zeal for hyperbole. Note how small becomes big, in the style of Neruda's watermelon images:

O packmule of the playground canyons,
Hairless llama of the tabletop mountains,
Unhumped camel of the sandlot deserts,
Undeterred by flying toes and grasping fingers,
Stubbornly avoiding ocean puddles,
Foraging through spear grass forests,
How magnificent your struggles,
How persistent your endeavors,

29

How laden your baggage . . .

The poem continues in this vein until its hilarious resolution:

O virtuous ant,
Would that I could find
an ant among men.

Neruda, who called bees a "fine, flashing proletariat," would have concurred.

One of the most gratifying opportunities presented by teaching the odes is the opportunity to witness students liberate themselves through humor. This sense of freedom—and behind it the subversive idea that students might actually enjoy poetry, might laugh and sing with it—is the essence of the Chilean bard. In this spirit, Kim Shable, a high school student from Aurora, Ohio, wrote "Ode to Daytime TV," with rhyming quatrains, no less: "Where would I be without daytime TV? / Probably somewhere worthwhile. / But hey, you know me! And I'm sure you'll agree / You can leave me with my Gomer Pyle." Some of the humor in odes by high school students is, of course, *adolescent.* One "Ode to Big Butt" comes to mind. I will not elaborate.

And what of the anti-ode, that poem disguised as an ode that actually condemns rather than celebrates? Neruda satirized all critics in his "Ode to Criticism":

some were partisans
of the king and his exalted monarchy,
others had been snared
in Marx's brow
and were kicking their feet in his beard,
some were English
plain and simply English,
and among them
they set out
with tooth and knife,
with dictionaries and other dark weapons,
with venerable quotes,
they set out
to take my poor poetry
from the simple folk
who loved it.

The anti-ode is handy for those students in no mood to praise anybody or anything, a useful alternative to the forced cheer that might otherwise prevail. One high school teacher in urban Springfield, Massachusetts, Paul Rieker, his vacation ruined by Amtrak, wrote an anti-ode to that beleaguered train system:

> Two hours tardy, a blacked-out string
> of coaches limping through Vermont evening,
> sans generator, sans lights, air conditioning and club car . . .
> The coach we were in was a black hole
> where my 133 dollars went. The conductor
> three times tried to read our tickets
> with his pin light as he caromed off
> the seats on both sides of the aisle while the
> train climbed the spine of Vermont and swayed
> jerkily over the rail bed. He finally gave up,
> saying: you look like honest people.

Needless to say, this poem was greeted in our workshop with furious applause.

The ode is a test of the poet's skill in the same way that the closing argument is a test of skill for the trial lawyer. How persuasive is the poet? Is the audience convinced of the subject's importance? This test is complicated where, as mentioned above, I challenge the class to write an ode on behalf of something I despise. Here I am not referring to a rational loathing, like my hatred of the Klan, but rather an irrational loathing, like my hatred of walnuts. As a result, I am now collecting odes to the walnut (Neruda's own contribution to the literature of ugly food is his "Ode to an Artichoke"). This ode to a walnut, written with hyberbolic humor and grace by David Shaffer, a high school teacher from Springfield, Massachusetts, is quoted here in its entirety:

Ode to a Walnut

> The wood of your tree
> contains all life
> from crib to coffin.
> A transfusion of your stain
> pumps life,
> makes grey ash and distressed pine
> into breathing, brown wood.

If my tongue touches your Midas bitterness,
my features are transmuted into your wrinkled clone.

O corrugated planet,
you in his palms
could soothe Captain Queeg to sanity.

Without you,
how textureless the brownie!
How still the pixie oar!

Paradigm of mystery:
rawhide Gordian knot
soaked and shriveled dry.

Fossilized testicle,
brain of a shrunken head,
you are all life,
you are all experience.

Ultimately, Neruda's odes inspire poetry because he is a great poet. His odes make connections between great and small, the momentary and the infinite. In his "Ode to Salt," with one phrase—"ola del salero" (which I translate as "wave of the saltshaker")—Neruda merges the vast ocean with grains of table salt, great and small on a continuum. We can taste "el sabor central del infinito" ("the essential taste of the infinite") in the salt of the table, if we can see the wave of the sea in the wave of the saltshaker. More extraordinary still, with Neruda's hand guiding us, we can teach others to write such poems. Or write them ourselves.

Bibliography

Selected Odes of Pablo Neruda. Translated by Margaret Sayers Peden. Berkeley, Calif.: University of California Press, 1990.

Neruda and Vallejo: Selected Poems. Translated by Robert Bly and James Wright. Boston, Mass.: Beacon, 1971.

KENNETH KOCH

Writing Poems Inspired by Lorca

First of all, read the following two poems by Federico García Lorca:

Romance sonambulo

Verde que te quiero verde.
Verde viento. Verdes ramas.
El barco sobre la mar
y el caballo en la montaña.
Con la sombra en la cintura
ella sueña en su baranda,
verde carne, pelo verde,
con ojos de fria plata.
Verde que te quiero verde.
Bajo la luna gitana,
las cosas la están mirando
y ella no puede mirarlas.

Verde que te quiero verde.
Grandes estrellas de escarcha
vienen con el pez de sombra
que abre el camino del alba.
La higuera frota su viento
con la lija de sus ramas,
y el monte, gato garduño,
eriza sus pitas agrias.
¿Pero quién vendrá? ¿Y por dónde . . . ?
Ella sigue en su baranda,
verde carne, pelo verde,
soñando en la mar amarga.

—Compadre, quiero cambiar
mi caballo por su casa,
mi montura por su espejo,

mi cuchillo por su manta.
Compadre, vengo sangrando,
desde los puertos de Cabra.
—Si yo pudiera, mocito,
este trato se cerraba.
Pero yo ya no soy yo,
ni mi casa es ya mi casa.
—Compadre, quiero morir
decentemente en mi cama.
De acero, si puede ser,
con las sábanas de holanda.
¿No ves la herida que tengo
desde el pecho a la garganta?
—Trescientas rosas morenas
lleva tu pechera blanca.
Tu sangre rezuma y huele
alrededor de tu faja.
Pero yo ya no soy yo,
ni mi casa es ya mi casa.
—Dejadme subir al menos
hasta las altas barandas;
dejadme subir!, dejadme,
hasta las verdes barandas.
Barandales de la luna
por donde retumba el agua.
Ya suben los dos compadres
hacia las altas barandas.
Dejando un rastro de sangre.
Dejando un rastro de lágrimas.
Temblaban en los tejados
farolillos de hojalata.
Mil panderos de cristal
herían la madrugada.
Verde que te quiero verde,
verde viento, verdes ramas.
Los dos compadres subieron.
El largo viento dejaba
en la boca un raro gusto
de hiel, de menta y de albahaca.
¡Compadre! ?Donde está, dime?
¿Donde está tu niña amarga?
¡Cuántas veces te esperó!

¡Cuántas veces te esperara,
cara fresca, negro pelo,
en esta verde baranda!

Sobre el rostro del aljibe
se mecía la gitana.
Verde carne, pelo verde,
con ojos de fría plata.
Un carambano de luna
la sostiene sobre el agua.
La noche se puso íntima
como una pequeña plaza.
Guardias civiles borrachos
en la puerta golpeaban.
Verde que te quiero verde.
Verde viento. Verdes ramas.
El barco sobre la mar.
Y el caballo en la montaña.

Sleepwalking Ballad

Green, how I want you green.
Green wind. Green branches.
The ship out on the sea
and the horse on the mountain.
With the shade around her waist
she dreams on her balcony,
green flesh, her hair green,
with eyes of cold silver.
Green, how I want you green.
Under the gypsy moon,
all things are watching her
and she cannot see them.

Green, how I want you green.
Big hoarfrost stars
come with the fish of shadow
that opens the road of dawn.
The fig tree rubs its wind
with the sandpaper of its branches,
and the forest, cunning cat,
bristles its brittle fibers.
But who will come? And from where?

She is still on her balcony
green flesh, her hair green,
dreaming in the bitter sea.

—My friend, I want to trade
my horse for her house,
my saddle for her mirror,
my knife for her blanket.
My friend, I come bleeding
from the gates of Cabra.
—If it were possible, my boy,
I'd help you fix that trade.
But now I am not I,
nor is my house now my house.
—My friend, I want to die
decently in my bed.
Of iron, if that's possible,
with blankets of fine chambray.
Don't you see the wound I have
from my chest up to my throat?
—Your white shirt has grown
three hundred dark brown roses.
Your blood oozes and flees
around the corners of your sash.
But now I am not I,
nor is my house now my house.
—Let me climb up, at least,
up to the high balconies;
Let me climb up! Let me,
up to the green balconies.
Railings of the moon
through which the water rumbles.

Now the two friends climb up,
up to the high balconies.
Leaving a trail of blood.
Leaving a trail of teardrops.
Tin bell vines
were trembling on the roofs.
A thousand crystal tambourines
struck at the dawn light.

Green, how I want you green,
green wind, green branches.
The two friends climbed up.
The stiff wind left
in their mouths a strange taste of bile, of mint, and of basil.
My friend, where is she—tell me—
where is your bitter girl?
How many times she waited for you!
How many times would she wait for you,
cool face, black hair,
on this green balcony!
Over the mouth of the cistern
the gypsy girl was swinging,
green flesh, her hair green,
with eyes of cold silver.
An icicle of moon
holds her up above the water.
The night became intimate
like a little plaza.
Drunken "Guardias Civiles"
were pounding on the door.
Green, how I want you green.
Green wind. Green branches.
The ship out on the sea.
And the horse on the mountain.

—*Translated by William Bryant Logan*

Arbole, arbole . . .

Arbole, arbole,
seco y verde.

La niña del bello rostro
está cogiendo aceituna.
El viento, galán de torres,
la prende por la cintura.
Pasaron cuatro jinetes
sobre jacas andaluzas,
con trajes de azul y verde,
con largas capas oscuras.
"Vente a Córdoba, muchacha."
La niña no los esucha.

37

Pasaron tres torerillos
delgaditos de cintura,
con trajes color naranja
y espadas de plata antigua.
"Vente a Sevilla, muchacha."
La niña no los escucha.
Cuando la tarde se puso
morada, con luz difusa,
pasó un joven que llevaba
rosas y mirtos de luna.
"Vente a Granada, muchacha."
Y la niña no lo escucha.
La niña del bello rostro
sigue cogiendo aceituna,
con el brazo gris del viento
ceñido por la cintura.
Arbole, arbole.
Seco y verde.

Tree, Tree . . .

Tree, tree
dry and green.

The girl with the pretty face
is out picking olives.
The wind, playboy of towers,
grabs her around the waist.
Four riders passed by
on Andalusian ponies,
with blue and green jackets
and big, dark capes.
"Come to Cordoba, muchacha."
The girl won't listen to them.
Three young bullfighters passed,
slender in the waist,
with jackets the color of oranges
and swords of ancient silver.
"Come to Seville, muchacha."
The girl won't listen to them.
When the afternoon had turned
dark brown, with scattered light,
a young man passed by, wearing

roses and myrtle of the moon.
"Come to Granada, muchacha."
And the girl won't listen to him.
The girl with the pretty face
keeps on picking olives
with the grey arm of the wind
wrapped around her waist.

Tree, tree.
Dry and green.

     —Translated by William Bryant Logan

~ ~ ~

For my elementary school classes, I chose these poems by Lorca because I felt their dreamy use of colors and their sense of magic places would appeal to children. I was drawn to the poems, too, because they are in Spanish, which gave me a chance to give my Spanish-speaking students some poetry in their language, and to heighten all my students' sense of the sound and color of words by having them compare, as they read, Spanish words with their English equivalents, and, when they wrote, having them use words in both languages. I suspect that many of the children hadn't ever really seen any poetry in another language. It was good to show them that there was such a thing, and to give them some idea of what a translation is.

I read the poems aloud, in English first; then as I went through the poems ("Arbole, arbole" and the first twenty-four lines of "Romance sonambulo," which seemed too long to go over in its entirety in class), along with explaining what was happening, I stopped at certain words or phrases to read them in Spanish as well as in English. I had the children close their eyes and listen, for example, to "*verde*" and "green," to "*verdes ramas*" and "green branches." I asked, "Which is greener? Which makes you see more leaves?" I did the same with "moon" and "*luna*," asking "Which is moonier? which is yellower? which more silvery?" The children answered enthusiastically, and by the time we had finished, they were excited about the sound of Spanish and English words. They were in a state to be thinking whether the sky outside the window was more blue or more *azul*, whether Aicza's dress was more orange or more *naranja*, whether, in fact, they'd prefer to be boys and girls or *niños* and *niñas*.

The assignment was: "Write a poem about a beautiful, strange place which is full of colors. Include some Spanish words in the poem. These may be color words, or any other words you find in the Lorca poems that

39

you would like to use because of what they mean or just because you like the way they look or sound—you don't have to know what they mean." It may help the children with form to tell them that they can, if they wish, put at least one color and one Spanish word in every line; or that they can put one Spanish word for a color (like *verde, plata,* or *naranja)* in every line. Some Spanish-speaking students asked if they could write their whole poems in Spanish, and Yuk asked me if instead of Spanish she could use Chinese. I agreed to both requests. Yuk wrote her poem out line by line in English, too; and when the all-Spanish poems were completed I had their authors translate them into English.

The excitement and good feeling a lesson like this creates in a class where many students know another language is something to see. There was a buzz as the Spanish-speaking students read over the Lorca poems, recognizing words and trying them out aloud; during the writing of the poems there was constant interchange between those children who knew Spanish and those who didn't, those who didn't asking for the meaning or pronunciation of words in the Lorca poems and also for Spanish words to fit an English meaning they had in mind. The Spanish-speaking children were very excited, too, about translating their poems—flipping their papers over, they got right to work and wrote quickly, obviously enjoying the minor magic of translation. They also especially enjoyed reading the Spanish works aloud.

My students created some fine vivid places, such as Lynne's Rainy Storm Palace and Antoinette's palace with a "window made of diamantes," Chip's completely blue (*azul*) world, Aicza's "planeta . . . de muchas colores," Mayra's green Mars, Andrew's world under green mist. Some color images were sharp and beautiful in the way Lorca's are, like Benny's "azul water with verde boats and azul people" and Rebecca's ducks on the lake next to a yellow flower. A few poems, such as Chip's and Damary's, picked up Lorca's theme of desire for a color.

I didn't say much about the ballad aspects—story and characters—of "Romance sonambulo," but a good lesson could be made by concentrating on those, too. The children could be asked to write a story poem, in which something dramatic happens, and to set the story in a strange place with many colors, and perhaps to give the characters and places Spanish names, using other Spanish words too if they wished. If the children like story poems, they might enjoy old English ballads, too, such as "Lord Randal" and "The Demon Lover."

The two poems in this section using French words were written by French-speaking students at the Newman School in New Orleans. Even when children don't know the language, a foreign language poem accompanied by a translation can make for a good class, because of the inspiration and excitement brought on by the sight and sound of the strange and beautiful words. I'd suggest, in fact, one class like this in any series of lessons.

FIFTH GRADE

Rojo rojo
¡Que bonito caballo!
Cuando miro al caballo rojo
Me da gana de llorar
Porque rojo rojo es un color maravilloso.

Red, red
What a pretty horse
When I look at my horse I feel
Like crying because red is a wonderful color.

¡Qué bonito gatito!
Cuando lo miro yo me da gracia
Porque el gatito es lindo.

What a pretty cat
When I look at him he makes me laugh
Because my cat is pretty

— *Jennie Ortiz*

Yo fui a un planeta y era de muchos colores y los colores eran blanco y verde. Eran bien bonitos. ¡Que lindos lindos eran los colores esos! A mi me paso una cosa. Me desnudé y me puse unas ropas de plata. Después me empecé a despertar. Otra vez me alegro a ver mi mamá y mis amigos y amigas y papá y hermanos y hermanas a mis pies.

I went to a planet and it was of lots of colors. They were white and green. They were very pretty. What pretty, pretty colors. Something happened to me. I took off my clothes and put on clothes made out of silver. I woke up. I was happy because I saw my mother, father, sisters, brothers, and friends.

—*Aicza Bermúdez*

The color yellow is like the sun.
El color amarillo es como el sol.

The color red makes me happy.
El color rojo me hace feliz.

The color green makes me feel good.
El color verde me hace sentir bien.

—*Carmen Berrios*

if the city was verde
and the sea was verde
and things were verde think how Miss Pitts would look in verde
and the sky was verde and a little rojo in the ground
Verde verde verde. I wish the sea was verde
The sea is verde are you verde.

—*Damary Hernández*

Verde looks like the water at night—azul water with verde boats and azul people.

—*Benny Vincifora*

Blue is the ocean
Nice is the sky
Huge are the buildings

Azul es el mar.
Lindo es el cielo.
¡Qué casas más lindas y grandes!

—*José Castillo*

Azul

Oh azul oh azul everything is azul from the tip of its tail to top of its nose it's azul everything it is azul but alas it turns Verde for the day's night but in the morning it will be azul again and I will come, it will be azul from the tip of its tail to top of its nose, yes It will be azul.

—*Chip Wareing*

Poem

At six o'clock the buildings seemed rojo.
At twelve o'clock the sky turned a beautiful azul.
It was time to dress up in verde.
My bet was lost because clay turned rojo.
And the sun became as yellow as a montaña de plata.
The blackboard is turning as blanco as his Sunday shirt.

> —*Kenneth Koch and Rosa Rosario*

Red, yellow, white, black, brown, pink.

紅 , 黃 , 白, 黑 , 棕 , 粉紅.

Green restaurant.

綠 飯 店.

Big red sun.

大 紅 太 陽

> —*Yuk Leung*

El sueño de la flor amarilla—The Dream of the Yellow Flower

Cuando el sol brilla la flor tiene más alumbración si no tiene agua la flor se muere los patitos nadan en el charco de agua se ven muy lindos al lado de una flor amarilla.

When the sun brightens the flower has brightness. If it doesn't have water it would die.

The ducks swim in a lake of water it looks so pretty next to a yellow flower.

> —*Rebecca Crespo*

Once when I went home it was boring so I went to a building that was being rebuilt
And I built myself a palace named after the beautiful queen Miss Pitts (she was an old devil with horns but I wanted to make her happy) herself with a verde baranda
And a plata montaña with walls of plata and oro

And a window made of diamantes and I had dresses made of the finest soles in
the land.
And all my friends would come and see me the queen.

—*Antoinette Anderson*

The City of Adventure

One day in the City of Verde there was a terrible fall of ramas. The gitana
crashed into the earth. All of the people ran to the plata house where they
were protected. There were no heaters in the plata house so the people died of
escarcha.

—*Steven Lenik*

In Rainy Storm Palace the estrellas are a pretty color of verde, the luna is a
pretty color of plata. The color of the people is amarillo, and the montañas
are very high y punta. Also the amarge is a pretty color of azul.

—*Lynne Reif*

Los hombres son el color verde y las mujers son el color amarillo y los
muchachos son el color verde y amarillo.

The men are the color green and the ladies are the color yellow and the children are the color green and yellow.

—*Wilson Pérez*

Los colores

La noche es negra como la oscuridad del mar.
El cielo es azul como el cielo.

—*Carmen Aponte*

SIXTH GRADE

Mars the Green Green Planet

Green wind. Green branches
Everything you see is green
Green snowflakes, green green songs
Will sing upon the green green hill.
Mañana tomorrow everything will turn azul and amarillo like the blue azul
sky.

I must go now.
Soon the green fades away and everything will vanish.

   —*Mayra Morales*

The World under Green Mist

Under the moon's green mist lie dreams of beauty and wonder
There are beds of fur from a fox
The warmth of the fireplace glows sparks of wonder
With the peaceful dark of the night lie fire bugs flickering their lights
Oh under this world with green mist lie the dreams of every person
Hidden from them until they die.

   —*Andrew Vecchione*

As I Sailed

The sea was amarillo
with waves of rojo
The sun azul
And the sky gris
This was all this
As I sailed In my verde boat.

   —*Sedley Alpaugh*

A verde mushroom
With a morado stem
Started to turn rojo
In the amarillo sun.

   —*Sedley Alpaugh*

I have a Persuvius
The only one on the block
His legs are wine color
Rouge with violet spots
His verte colored neck
Flashes in the noir sun
He flows along the ground in a blanc stream.

   —*Author unknown*

By the azul lake and the azure sky,
A small morado poppy stood

With a blanco dewdrop on its head.
The waves rippled and the verde grass rippled
While the morado poppy swayed back and forth.
The waves hit the cafe ground
And covered the poppy and the verde grass,
Burying and killing them both.

 —*Melanie Myers*

La grenouille est verte
Pourquoi?
Le coq est orange
Pourquoi?
Le lapin est brun
Pourquoi?
Pourquoi je suis une couleur?

 —*Stephen Godchaux*

The Thing

In a way the thing was morado,
But yet there was a touch of azul shining here and there
It seemed as though I saw a sliver of amarillo shining
Like a diamond in a negro night
The rojo color in it was as rojo as a sports car and
Still as blanco as a naranja sky.

 —*Susan Strug*

Lorca for High School and College Students

The Moon Rises

When the moon comes up
the bells are lost
and there appear
impenetrable paths.

   When the moon comes up
the sea blankets the earth
and the heart feels
like an island in infinity.

   No one eats oranges
under the full moon.
One must eat
cold green fruit.

   When the moon comes up
with a hundred equal faces,
silver money
sobs in the pocket.

   —*Translated by William Bryant Logan*

Ballad of Luna, Luna

The moon came to the forge
with her petticoat of spikenard.
The boy looks and looks at her.
The boy is looking at her.
In the whirling air
the moon moves her arms
and shows off, slick and pure,
her breasts of hard tin.

—Run luna, luna, luna.
If the Gypsies should come
they'd make of your heart
necklaces and white rings.
—Child, let me dance.
When the Gypsies come
they'll find you over the anvil
with your eyelids closed.
—Run luna, luna, luna,
for now I can hear their horses.
—Child, let me alone. Don't stamp
on my starched whiteness.

The rider came closer,
playing on the drum of the plain.
Inside the forge, the boy
has his eyes closed.

Through the olive grove,
bronze and dreaming, came the Gypsies.
Their heads upraised
and their eyes half-closed.
How the tawny owl sings,
oh, how it sings in the tree!
Through the sky goes the moon
with a boy by the hand.

Inside the forge the Gypsies
cry, letting out shrieks.
The wind is watching, watching it.
The wind is watching over it.

   —Translated by William Bryant Logan

Little Viennese Waltz

In Vienna there are ten young girls,
a shoulder on which death is sobbing,
and a forest of stuffed doves.
There's a fragment of the morning
in the frost's museum.
There's a salon with a thousand windows.
  Ay, ay, ay, ay!
Take this waltz with your mouth shut.

This waltz, this waltz, this waltz,
of itself and of cognac and death,
that dips its gown's tail in the sea.

I love you, I love you, I love you,
with the dead book and the easy chair,
down the melancholy hallway,
in the lily's dark loft,
in our own bed of the moon,
and in the dance the tortoise dreams.
Ay, ay, ay, ay!
Take this waltz bent at the waist.

There are in Vienna four mirrors
where your mouth and the echoes play.
There's a death for pianoforte
that paints the young boys blue.
There are beggars on the rooftops.
There are fresh bouquets of cries.
Ay, ay, ay, ay!
Take this waltz which is dying in my arms.

Because I love you, my love, I love you
in the loft where the children play,
dreaming of the old lights of Hungary
through the noises of the weak afternoon,
watching the sheep and the lilies of snow
on the dark silence of your brow.
Ay, ay, ay, ay!
Take this "I'll love you forever" of a waltz.

In Vienna I'll dance with you
in a costume with
a river's head.
Look what hyacinth banks I have!
I'll leave my mouth between your legs,
my soul in white lilies and photographs,
and in the dark waves of your walking
I want, my love, my love, to leave,
violin and sepulcher, the ribbons of the waltz.

—*Translated by William Bryant Logan*

Dawn

Dawn in New York comes
with four columns of slime
and a hurricane of doves
splattering in the stagnant water.

Dawn in New York wails
on the huge stairways
searching among the angles
for spikenards of haggard pain.

Dawn comes and no one takes her in his mouth
because there there's no chance of morning or hope.
Sometimes the coins in mad swarms
slam into and devour abandoned children.

The first to come out know in their bones
that there will be no paradise, no lovers stripped of leaves;
they know they're going to the slime of numbers and laws,
to the games without art, to the sweats without issue.

The light is buried by chains and noise
shamelessly defying a science with no roots.
There are people staggering through the suburbs unable to sleep
as if they'd just escaped a shipwreck of blood.

—Translated by William Bryant Logan

Song of the Black Cubans

When the full moon rises
I'll go to Santiago de Cuba.
I'll go to Santiago
in a black water car.
I'll go to Santiago.
The palm leaf roofs will sing.
I'll go to Santiago.
When the palm tree wants to be a stork.
I'll go to Santiago.
And the banana tree a jellyfish.
I'll go to Santiago.
With Fonseca's blond head.
I'll go to Santiago.
And Romeo and Juliet's rose.

I'll go to Santiago.
Paper sea and coin silver.
I'll go to Santiago.
Oh Cuba, oh rhythm of dry seeds!
I'll go to Santiago.
Oh hot waist and drop of wood!
I'll go to Santiago.
Harp of living tree trunks,
cayman, tobacco flower!
I'll go to Santiago.
I always said I'd go to Santiago
in a black water car.
I'll go to Santiago.
Alcohol and breeze in the wheels.
I'll go to Santiago.
My coral in the darkness.
I'll go to Santiago.
The sea drowned in the sand.
I'll go to Santiago.
White heat, dead fruit.
I'll go to Santiago.
Oh bovine freshness of reeds!
Oh Cuba! Oh curve of sighs and clay!
I'll go to Santiago.

—*Translated by William Bryant Logan*

About Lorca

The Spanish poet Federico García Lorca spent some time in New York and in Cuba when he was in his early thirties. In 1936, when he was thirty-seven, Lorca was killed by the fascists during the Spanish Civil War. His early poems, written in Andalusia, where he was born, are often like strange folk tales or fairy tales—sometimes stories about nature, sometimes about the lives of the gypsies. The poems written in New York are rougher and freer and less songlike and have other subjects.

Lorca's poetry is always wild and strange in one way or another. There are mysterious places and unexplainable things and extraordinary events. There is a forest of stuffed doves, a salon with a thousand windows, a paper sea, a black water car. Money "sobs in the pocket," the New York dawn has "four columns of slime," the "palm tree wants to be a stork." Lorca's way of writing makes everything he writes about seem mysterious and strange.

You are probably used to the way a place, for instance the town you live in, looks completely different to you depending on your mood, your feelings. One day it is beautiful; another day it is horrible. What is inside you always changes what is outside you. In his poetry Lorca doesn't try to separate what he is feeling from what is outside him. Instead, he seems to allow what he is feeling and thinking to transform what is around him. Lorca doesn't say that the sea with moonlight on it is like a "paper sea and coin silver," but simply that a paper and coin sea exists and is there. The longed-for coast of Cuba is a "curve of sighs and clay." And he doesn't say, "I want so much to go to Cuba that it seems to me that even the trees are full of longing—the palm tree, for instance, looks as if it wants to be able to fly, to be a stork." Instead he says, "The palm tree wants to be a stork." Sometimes Lorca just makes little lists of things, not even taking time to connect them: "Oh Cuba, oh rhythm of dried seeds! . . . Harp of living tree trunks, cayman, tobacco flower . . . Alcohol and breeze in the wheels." When Lorca wrote this way, it's unlikely that first he got the feelings and then found words to fit them. It's more likely that words and feelings occurred simultaneously. Imagine, for instance, that you're looking out the window and, without knowing why, you think about coins. If you're in one mood you might write, as Lorca does in "The Moon Rises," "silver money/ sobs in the pocket." If you're in another mood, you might write, as he does in "Dawn," "Sometimes the coins in mad swarms / slam into and devour abandoned children." Both descriptions are very complicated and dramatic combinations of what is really there and what is in one's feelings. They are not realistic descriptions; they are not descriptions that you are likely to arrive at intellectually. One reason for writing in such an unrealistic and indirect way is that you can get to the strong and complex and strange kind of truth that there is, for instance, in your dreams.

Lorca thought that this kind of truth, this kind of poetry, was inspired by something he called the *duende,* a dark, overwhelming source of inspiration. The *duende* doesn't inspire gentle, intellectual poetry, but strong, dark, and passionate poetry, poetry that stays always a little mysterious and beyond you.

≈ ≈ ≈

You may wonder, in writing so unrealistically, how you can ever tell when what you say is good or "right." The answer is that it's good when it sounds right, when it feels right, when, as you read it over, you feel convinced and excited—you may even catch your breath. This feeling of rightness will have to do with the sounds of the words, with their meanings, with their associations for you, with how they're used together. As you write poetry, you begin to understand this, but it's probably impossible to explain completely, nor do you really need to understand it in order to write in that way.

You may not at the moment or even in the next few days be filled with the *duende,* but it's interesting to try being deliberately unrealistic, as Lorca is. A good kind of poem for this is one like "Song of Black Cubans," Lorca's strange, dreamlike description of Santiago. You could choose some amazing-seeming and desirable, maybe even dangerously exciting, place to write about—and describe it in a way that may be true only for you, whatever you dream of or imagine its being like. Just start writing. If you deliberately try to fill the place with impossible things, if you make it all unreal, it will probably turn out to be real in another way, real in the way Lorca's poems are. Think of the streets and of the weather and of how the men and women are dressed. Maybe there are fountains or Ferris wheels, fireworks, strange birds. Think of the flowers and the mud and the grass and the trees, the vehicles, the lightning and thunder, the kind of music there is, the animals, the birds, and always the colors of things, the taste, the sound, the touch. A good kind of place to inspire such a poem may be a tropical city, like the Santiago Lorca writes about—a man-made and bright-colored place but with wild nature all around it, a place where you might find violent heat, palm trees filled with birds out the window, maybe even lions roaming through the hotels. You might begin by thinking of a city name that gives you the feeling of such a place—perhaps Bogota, Acapulco, Coronado, Andalusia, Cuzco, Tongaville—or make up an exotic name. Like Lorca, you might keep saying you are going to this place and keep repeating its name—"I am going to Chichicaslenango." Say in each line or in every other line what will be there, what you will see, what you will do, how you will get there, what the animals, birds, and highways there are doing, what they want, what is bursting forth and shining there, how the balconies feel and the flowers in the people's hands. Use Lorca-like lists and, if you like, his strange combinations using the word *of*—"harp of living tree trunks," "curve of sighs and clay."

MARK STATMAN

Waiting, Listening, and Wondering

Using Three Poems by Mayra Jiménez, Homero Aridjis, and Ernesto Cardenal

1. Mayra Jiménez

Ayer
los árboles
las flores
y las pequeñas yerbas
se movían
tal vez todavía estén
moviéndose
mientras yo te esperaba
con inquietud
en el parque
temiendo ser sorprendida
por alguien conocido;
pero tú no llegaste
y apareció la noche
ampliamente
aunque lenta
en medio de la gente
que iba y venía
quién sabe a qué dolor
mientras yo allí
parecía una extraña
con una rama
en la mano

—*Mayra Jiménez*

Yesterday
the trees
the flowers
and the small grasses
moved
perhaps they still are
moving
while I waited for you
worried
in the park
afraid of being surprised
by someone I knew;
but you didn't come
and the night appeared
grew
though slowly
in the middle of people
who went and came
who knows to what pain
while I stood there
a stranger
with a branch
in my hand

   —*Translated by Mark Statman*

Over the last seven or eight years, I've had a good time teaching this poem
by Mayra Jiménez, the Venezuelan-born poet who lives in Costa Rica and
whom I first met in 1987 in Nicaragua. At the time, along with Ernesto
Cardenal, who was Minister of Culture, Mayra was coordinating and teaching in the literacy brigades which worked throughout the country, using
poetry as a way to teach children and adults how to read and write.

Jiménez's poem describes a situation that students of all ages can understand. Someone is waiting, hoping, for something to happen. They
know what it means to be in the middle of anticipating, the combination
of excitement (what they can imagine) and boredom (how slowly the clock
moves). They're also interested in the fact that the poet doesn't get what she
wants: she's been stood up by someone. She's upset. She doesn't want to be
seen by anybody who knows her because she's embarrassed at the idea that
someone has done this to her. They understand that she projects her feelings onto everyone and everything around her ("who went and came / who

knows to what pain") and the students can talk about how they've done that themselves. We also spend a good deal of time talking about how mysterious the last line is. What is that branch in her hand? I once had a student suggest she was going use it to beat the person, should the person ever arrive. Others have suggested that it's an olive branch, for reconciliation. Others that it's the stem of a flower whose petals have all dropped away.

I like to teach this poem, too, because of its attention to language and emotional details. The poem is about waiting and hoping, and about the sadness and pain that comes with not getting what you've waited and hoped for. The imagery and word choice go a long way toward creating that mood. The grasses are small, nothing is moving, and when the night appears, it does so slowly, drawing out the difficulty of the moment. The trees and flowers are not described, they have no color, there is nothing beautiful about them. They are separate from the poet, serving only as one more way for the poet to think about how she feels.

Sometimes I ask the students to imagine the poem Mayra might have written had the person arrived. I ask them to think about what kinds of details she might have been used to show happiness—what kinds of colors, what words. I'll ask them, too, to think about the skinniness of the poem, which is suggestive of its bleakness. How would fat lines or a combination of fat and thin, or other kinds of word placements affect the mood?

When I ask the students to write, I ask them to focus on the time of waiting, of hoping, and not the time of meeting or receiving. This gives them a chance to examine the complexity of the emotions they feel during that time. Often—and this is something we talk about—the waiting/hoping time is the time that's most physically and emotionally compelling; what comes next is anti-climactic. Sometimes the idea of waiting/hoping takes them in directions I couldn't have anticipated:

nosotros somos bebés
después somos medianos
después somos grandes
después somos señores
después somos viejitos
y después nos morimos
los días pasan rápidos
como los conejos

   —*Wilbert Miranda, third grade*

we are babies
then we are medium
then we are big
then we are adults
then we are old
and then we die
the days pass quickly
like rabbits

    —Translated by Mark Statman

I play with snow
It is shaped with beauty
You see the people you know
The soup waits to be eaten
It is a perfect time to play
The white glistening snow glistens
through the day

It waits to be played in
Have your snowball fights
Have your fun
To me this is a wonder

    —Christina Pawlowski, third grade

While I Sat There and Waited

Yesterday it was dark and black
    in the sky

While in my house, I waited
walking angrily

Afraid of telling somebody
    that you have not called
The black trees swing back and
    forth
While I wait angrily for
    you to call
Meanwhile there I was
    a stranger
        in my own house
My feelings trapped inside of me

I could not tell you
how I felt
        on the phone

—*Adrienne Ricks, fifth grade*

The Letter

Lisette
you left me waiting for you at
the beach
The sand went through my toes
while I walked
I sat on a rock while the sun
was
setting and the birds flying
through
It wasn't like when we were kids
Now you're gone
I hope you write back love you
forever

(I dedicate this poem to my best
friend, Lisette Vásquez)

—*Jahida Rodríguez, fifth grade*

Difference/Waiting

There is nothing to do
There is nothing to see
Just a plain wall
No color or form
I hear the thin air
No response

—*Alex Balsam, sixth grade*

≈ ≈ ≈

2. Homero Aridjis

Hay silencio en la lluvia

hay silencio en la lluvia que cae estripitosamente sobre

el techo de lámina
en nuestro pensamiento hay silencio
en medio del ruido externo a veces estamos sumergidos en
el más profundo silencio y cuando de pronto un sonido
nos arranca de nuestra quietud se nos hace insoportable
toda voz y todo lo que nos llama nos rompe
sin embargo a veces rodeados de silencio parecemos estar
llenos de ruido los pensamientos suenan las manos suenan
el aire crepita y el más dulce rostro es altisonante

    el espacio se vuelve una enorme caja de resonancia
donde golpea sin cesar el tiempo, pero tambíen ocurre
que al hablar la voz no suena aunque lo pensado
parece arañar los vidrios

    —Homero Aridjis

There's Silence in the Rain

there's silence in the rain that pounds
against the tin roof
in our thoughts there's silence
in the middle of all the clamor around us
sometimes we're deep down in the heaviest silence
when suddenly a noise tears us away from our stillness
each voice is unbearable
everything that calls us tears us apart
on the other hand
we're sometimes surrounded by silence
and seem to be filled with noise
our thoughts make a sound our hands make a sound
the air crackles and the sweetest face
is a shrill note
    space becomes a huge sound box
where the hours beat away ceaselessly
yet at the same time what happens is that
the voice upon speaking doesn't sound
even though what it thought to say
seemes to be scratching at the windows

    —Translated by John Brandi

There's something very powerful about this poem by the Mexican poet and novelist, Homero Aridjis, who tries to characterize silence, to name it by describing how it can appear in our lives. The poem talks about the idea of hearing silence, of how, because of the absence of sound or because there is so much sound, silence can be so loud because we notice it so completely. This silence forces Aridjis inside his own head: What are these voices? Why are they saying these things? He raises questions about the connection between sound and space and about the way our minds understand and connect the inner sounds (we can hear ourselves think but there are no sound waves registered) to outer sounds (the ones we notice or screen out).

The week before I teach this poem, I try to get the kids to spend some time thinking about silence. I ask them to try to experience listening to silence. They can do this at home, outside, or in school. I ask them to think about the difference between silence in the day and silence in the night, as well as the difference between quiet and silence. I also ask them to spend some time listening to the voices and sounds they can hear in their heads, and to think about why they're able to hear these things even though no words are being spoken or sounds actually being made.

The day we read the poem, we spend some time trying to make the classroom as silent as possible. Usually we have to try this several times before we get the best results (at first, there's too much movement of chairs, tapping of pencils, coughing, laughing). Then we talk about what we heard in the silence. After this, we read Aridjis's poem and talk about his ideas. Additionally, I point out the richness of his language, how specifically he describes things. We also talk about his free-verse line and the way that this meditative kind of line contrasts with how much commotion there seems to be in the poem. Then I ask the kids to write their own silence poems.

> I see green boys and girls
> A sunny day
> but the sun is not out
> Everybody is sad
> and it was raining on the people
> and the people were crying
> and put on sad music
>
>   *—Shonette Trotter, first grade*

> When I am sleeping
> in the bed
> I hear rain
> I hear wind
> I hear people
> walking home
>
>   *—Ismail Abdur, first grade*

The World of Silence
World of
the night holds
mischief
brings to light
all things not seen
World of night
is a
candle slowly dripping and
falling
Of the night
The silence of mysteries
gather moistness fear
and unseen
Infinity
never to
end until breaks of sunlight
the mysteries of the
moon.
Shadows the features
of the darkness of the fields
Emerald fields glow
in the shines of stars
its counseling God Moon
Follows its footsteps
The moon lights
impenetrable paths as the sun sobs
its heart out
coldness of
night brings to life
the dead the dead whose
features represent the night
The glow of
the moon
loveliness overwhelming
brings the
sun
to an end
weeping
jealous, rage to kill not
strong enough
stars

show up one by
one
A child who
is lost in admiration of
the
coming of the moon
sets over the
plain
The sun comes up
and all is lost

—*Jenny Arthungal, fourth grade*

≈ ≈ ≈

3. Ernesto Cardenal

En el lago de Nicaragua

Media noche, en una lancha, en medio lago
entre San Miguelito y Granada.
Todavía no se ven las luces de Granada
y ya no se ven las lucecitas de San Miguelito.
Sólo las estrellas
(el mástil apuntando a las Siete Cabritas)
y la luna saliendo sobre Chontales.

Pasa otra lancha (una luz roja)
y se hunde en la noche.
Nosotros para ellos,
otra luz roja que se hunde en la noche . . .

Y yo acostado sobre cubierta mirando las estrellas
entre racimos de platanos y quesos chontaleños
pienso: tal vez una de ellas es otra tierra como ésta
y alguien me mira desde allí (mirando las estrellas)
desde otra lancha en mitad de otro lago.

—*Ernesto Cardenal*

On Lake Nicaragua

Midnight, on a boat, in the middle of the lake
between San Miguelito and Granada.

Already the lights from Granada are gone
and the ones at San Miguelito unseen.
Only the stars
(the mast points at the Seven Goats)
   and the moon setting over Chontales.

Another boat passes (a red light)
and disappears in the night.
We, for them,
   are another red light disappearing in the night . . .

And I'm lying on the covers and looking at the stars
lying between bunches of bananas and cheese from Chontales
thinking: perhaps one of them is another planet like this
and someone watches me from there (watching the stars)
from another boat in the middle of another lake.

   —Translated by Mark Statman

I like the way the wondering in this poem happens. When the narrator sees another boat's light (though not the boat), it makes him wonder about expectations and perceptions. He assumes the boat is a boat because of the light. The people on that boat could be speculating too. And this line of thinking continues when he looks at the sky and wonders: Is that star really a star? Maybe it's a planet and on that planet is a person in a boat in a lake looking at the sky, seeing a planet, wondering if someone is watching and wondering about what is there in the sky. Is someone looking at me looking at him looking at me?

Before I teach this poem, I ask the kids to think about wondering. I ask them what it means to wonder: Why do we do it? When do we do it? How? I ask them what they've wondered about in their lives. And we talk about how being certain places affects how they wonder, how it presents different kinds of things to think about and different ways to think about them. I'll ask them what the difference is, for example, between wondering at school and wondering at the beach, or between wondering in the woods and wondering in their bedrooms. We also talk about time as a factor: what's the difference between wondering in the middle of the night and the middle of the day? Between dawn and dusk?

Then we read and talk about the Cardenal poem, and I ask them to write their own wondering poems. I remind them of the importance of establishing the setting of the poem, that they should be as descriptive as possible in describing the where and when, so that the reader understands more than simply what they are wondering about.

In the night
the owls are lost
people gaze at the moon
watching meteors on
the sky. Their mittens
are catching fire. When
the dog looks at the
moon and then jumps
the cat is scared of
the fire balls in the
sky. A pond falls out
of the sky. The sky
becomes dark and gray.
The people think the
Lord has gone mad.

—*Justin Steinmann, third grade*

The Star of the Night

It looks like silk
a silk star
Two half moons all stuck
together, glowing like a
firefly in the sky
in the dark dark woods
to be king

—*Reuben Petty, third grade*

Leaves Are Dying

The leaves are dying water is clear
ducks quacking in the air.
Water moves a lovely way, winds
are blowing left and right.
Leaves are floating in the air gently over and over.
Water is peaceful, rising to the sun.

Ducks quacking, birds are flying.
There is a house across the lake.
The sun is shining such a beautiful color.

Leaves are dying and plants are growing. I wonder why is Nature
still this way. The leaves fall.
Fish swim to the opening sky.
Fish that died return
to their watery grave.
Squirrels run freely through branches of trees.
The leaves drop and die.

—*Junior Griffiths, fifth grade*

Bibliography

Aridjis, Homero. "Hay silencio . . . / There's silence" in *Un ojo en el muro / An Eye in the Wall*. Santa Fe, N.M.: Tooth of Time Books, 1986.

Cardenal, Ernesto. "En el lago de Nicaragua" in *Antologia de la poesía hispanoamericano*. Madrid: Selecciones Austral / Espasa Calipe, 1984.

Jiménez, Mayra. "Ayer" in *Cuando poeta*. Heredia, Costa Rica: Editorial de la Universidad Nacional.

To You / For You, Para Ti
Using a Poem by Miguel Hernández

Probably half the poems ever written were either to someone or with someone specific in mind. Love poems are the first thing we think of, but there are other messages as well: of comradery, anger, sadness, homesickness. I tell my students the trick to writing a To You / For You poem is to zero in on someone for whom you have real feelings, be they love, confusion, tenderness, whatever; then you have to have something to say, even if it's just to express how you feel.

To help us ease into the subject, I write three choices on the board:

1) (the easiest) to someone who died or went away.

I point out that just because a person is not physically present does not mean there is no longer a relationship. I tell them even though my mother died, she is still my mother; if something comes up in my mind to say to her, I say it. By the nods of agreement, I see a few students have experienced some kind of loss of their own.

2) to someone you can't say this to, face to face, for whatever reason.

Sometimes we are constrained by manners; sometimes it's considered inappropriate for kids to address their elders directly with the truth; sometimes we are simply shy. The great thing about a poem like this is that it matters tremendously that you get it out, whether you actually send it to the person or not.

3) to someone you feel you know, because of who they are or what they've done.

A lot of writers write poems to other writers—even if they lived in another century—because they've learned something or been touched in some way by what they've read. If you have a favorite writer, or singer, chances are that he or she is addressing issues that are important to you. You could almost say it seems they are speaking directly to you. This is the perfect time to write back. Or you may have someone you admire because you've watched them play ball, or you've studied how they act or dance, or perhaps you are impressed with their character.

First you have to decide who the person is that you'll be writing to, then what your message will be. Try to get some specific description of your person in the poem—either who they are internally, or how they appear to the outside world. "Dear Grandma, I really miss you" isn't half as strong as "I miss your wrinkled face and precious hands."

For the reader to feel something, he or she needs something to work with. If your message is written in emotional shorthand, like the way we speak, it may mean something to you and that person, but the rest of us will be in the dark. "Dear Susan, I will never forgive you for what you did!" We don't even know who Susan is, let alone what she did.

Or how about this? "Dear Michael Jordan: I love the way you play. Signed, A Fan." Maybe you do love how he plays, but you haven't convinced us. What do you love? How he seems to hang in mid-air, how he seems to fly? Do you love how he cared about his father? Put some of your observations of him in the poem.

Before we start with the Spanish poet, Miguel Hernández's "Nanas de la Cebolla" ("Lullabies of the Onion"), I tell them Miguel was a shepherd boy from a little village in Spain; he educated himself and had his first poems published in local papers. When he was twenty-two, his first book of poems came out, and he moved to the big city of Madrid. Three years later, just after his second book was published, the Spanish Civil War began. Franco, the dictator, was fighting with his soldiers and Civil Guard against the people. Hernández immediately volunteered to fight against Franco, and joined the Republican Army.

Back home, his girlfriend Josefina's father fought on Franco's side, and was killed in battle. Hernández offered to support her family, even though he was completely broke. Separated by the war, it took a year for Miguel and Josefina to get married. During the war he wrote another book; they saw each other whenever they could, and Josefina got pregnant. At the end of 1939, he was captured by Franco's forces and thrown into prison. Within a year he had tuberculosis.

After an operation, he wrote to Josefina, asking her to send him bandages and gauze, since there were no medical supplies in prison. At the very same time, she was writing to him, telling him that because of the war there was nothing to buy in the market but onions. Bread and onions was all she and their son had to live on. When he received that letter, Miguel wrote the "Lullabies of the Onion" to his son, whom he never saw again. Shortly after writing the poem, he died.

I tell this story as I work my way around the room, giving everyone a photocopy of the poem in Spanish and English, along with other To You / For You poems by kids. Hernández's poem, comprised of twelve stanzas, is too long to be read in its entirety in a forty-minute period. I've excerpted the five stanzas below. The poem can be found in Spanish, with English translation, in *Selected Poems of Miguel Hernández and Blas de Otero*.

From Nanas de la cebolla

La cebolla es escarcha
cerrada y pobre.
Escarcha de tus días
y de mis noches.
Hambre y cebolla,
hielo negro y escarcha
grande y redonda.

En la cuna del hambre
mi niño estaba.
Con sangre de cebolla
se amamantaba.
Pero tu sangre,
escarchada de azúcar,
cebolla y hambre.

Una mujer morena
resuelta en luna
se derrama hilo a hilo
sobre la cuna.
Ríete, niño,
que te traigo la luna
cuando es preciso.

Alondra de mi casa,
ríete mucho.
Es tu risa en tus ojos
la luz del mundo.
Ríete tanto
que mi alma al oirte
bata de espacio.

Desperté de ser niño:
nunca despiertes.
Triste llevo la boca:
ríete siempre.
Siempre en la cuna,
defendiendo la risa
pluma por pluma.

    —*Miguel Hernández*

From Lullabies of the Onion

The onion is frost
closed in and poor.
Frost of your days
and of my nights.
Hunger and onion,
black ice and frost
big and round.

In the cradle of hunger
my child was lying.
He was nursed with
the blood of the onion.
But it was your blood,
frosted with sugar,
onion and hunger.

A brown-skinned woman
turned into the moon
pours herself thread by thread
over the cradle.
Laugh, child,
I will bring you the moon
when it's time.

Lark of my house,
laugh often.
The laughter in your eyes
is the light of the world.
Laugh so much
that my soul, hearing you
will beat violently in space.

I woke up from being a child:
don't ever wake up.
My mouth is sad:
you keep on laughing.
In your cradle forever,
defending your laughter
feather by feather.

—Translated by Janine Pommy Vega

I ask the class to point out the strong description that makes us feel something. What is the feeling? Someone says love, another sadness, another tenderness. Which one of the choices on the board would it be? Someone tells us it's the first, because Hernández's son is not physically present. Someone else may suggest it could also be sadness because Hernández hasn't spent much time with his son, and most of what he knows he gets from his wife's letters.

I ask for volunteers to read the following poems in Spanish, then others to read them in English. (All except two of the poems in this essay were written in Spanish and translated by me into English. "Why I'm Punished" and "To the Serbs' President, Radovan Karadic" were written in English. I translated them into Spanish.) This exercise works well with students from fourth through at least twelfth grade. Through the course of a residency I try to get every member of a bilingual class to read aloud in English at least once. There is a shyness in approaching a language that seems to have as many rules for pronunciation as it has words. Even a rowdy bilingual junior high school class becomes quiet and concentrated when someone is reading aloud in English.

The following two poems are good examples of a message one can't say face to face.

La castigada

Estoy enojada contigo
por lo que pasó
y lo que hiciste.

Ellos no sabían nada
acerca de nosotros,
mis padres, mis tíos,
nadie sabía.

Yo iba a decirles,
pero tú me dijiste de no hacerlo.
Luego hablaste a tus amigos
de nosotros
y ellos hablaban delante
de mis tíos.

Ahora ellos no quieren hablar
conmigo,
y tú no me quieres hablar—
¿En serio, qué debo hacer?

    —Clara Quiñones, ninth grade

Why I'm Punished

I'm angry with you
because of what happened
and what you did.

They didn't know about us,
my parents, uncles,
nobody knew.

I was going to tell them,
but you told me not to.
Then you talked about us
to your friends
and they talked in front
of my uncles.

Now they won't talk to me,
you won't talk to me—
Really, what should I do?

Mi amiga Raquel

Tus ojos son negros
como un anochecer
Pero tu corazón brilla
en la oscuridad.

Tienes la piel canela
y tu corazón es limpio como
un niño que acaba de nacer.

Limpio como una rosa roja
que tienes en el jardín
Eres un corderito blanco
que juega hasta el amanecer.

Amanecer que nos trae
nuevas esperanzas,
mi dulce amiga,
Raquel.

       —Nalda Castillo, sixth grade

My Friend Raquel

Your eyes are dark
like nightfall
but your heart shines
in the darkness.

You have cinnamon-colored
skin, and your heart is clean
like a newborn child.

Clean like a red rose
that you have in the garden
You are a little white lamb
that plays until dawn.

Dawn that brings us
new hopes,
my sweet friend,
Raquel.

The next poems fall under the "Someone in your life who died or went away" category.

Querida Bisabuela

Yo quiero volver a verte,
querida bisabuela,
Sin tu presencia
la casa está
enormemente vacía.

Me hace falta tu carita
plegada, tus manos

preciosas
y tus consejos.

¿Qué voy hacer
sin tí?

      —Yudelka Gómez, seventh grade

Dear Great-Grandmother

I want to see you again,
dear Great-grandmother.
Without your presence
the house
is enormously empty.

I miss your little
wrinkled face, your
precious hands,
and your advice.

What am I going to do
without you?

Querida Madre

Querida madre
que te has ido
como el viento
y mi casa es
un sendero
perdido sin ti.

Todos te extrañamos,
tú eras mi guía,
mi todo. La vida
no parece igual
sin ti.

Me siento solo
y aunque a veces sonrío
mi corazón llora
Te extrañaré mucho,
Mamá.

      —Juan Abreú, eighth grade

Dear Mother

Dear Mother
you have gone
like the wind
and my house is
a lost path
without you.

We all miss you,
you were my guide,
my everything. Life
does not seem the same
without you.

I feel alone, and
even though I smile sometimes
my heart is crying
I will miss you a lot,
Mama.

Speaking to someone you feel you know because of who they are or
what they've done is illustrated by the following:

Al Presidente Serbo, Radovan Karadic

Sólo quiero decirte,
¡Qué vergüenza! ¿Qué hiciste?
¿Cuál fue la razón para matar
a mi niñez? ¿Cuál fue la razón
para romper mi sueño de niña?
¿Por qué trataste de matarme
cuando yo tenía solamente catorce años?
¿Por qué me diste la oscuridad
en mi ojo derecho?
Quiero decirte
cuanto te odio, y créeme,
mucha gente te odia
porque intentaste apagar
las luces en nuestras vidas, intentaste
matarme cuando tenía solamente
catorce años. ¡Qué vergüenza!

—*Mirela Kerla, eleventh grade ESL*

To the Serbs' President, Radovan Karadic

I just want to tell you,
Shame on you! What did you do?
What was the reason to kill
my childhood? What was the reason
to break my child's dream?
Why did you try to kill me
when I was just fourteen years old?
Why did you give me darkness
in my right eye?
I want to tell you
how much I hate you, and trust me,
a lot of people do
Because you tried to turn off
the lights in our lives, you tried
to kill me when I was
just fourteen. Shame on you!

A Selena

Alguien se ha llevado una estrella
del cielo sin pensar lo necesaria
que era.
Era una luz que brillaba y en sus ojos
se veía el amor que guardaba.

Es imposible pensar que te has ido
y nunca volverás
por culpa de un mal momento
y la persona sin sentimiento
decidió darte fin. Pero aunque
te hayas ido, nunca se ocupará
un lugar en tu nido. Siempre
brillarás en nuestro corazón.

Estrella, estrella siempre serás.

—Yesenia Cruz, tenth grade

To Selena

Someone has taken away a star
from the sky without thinking
how necessary you were.
You were a light that shined
and in your eyes could be seen
the love that you held.

It's impossible to think
that you've gone and will
never return
because of one evil moment
and the person without feelings
who decided to end your life.
But though you have gone, no one
will occupy a space in your nest.
You will always shine in our heart.

A star, a star you will always be.

A variation of the To You / For You poem that works well in bilingual and ESL classes, where the students have recently arrived from a country that is still fresh in their hearts and memories, is a direct address to the homeland. I sometimes substitute this possibility for one of the others. Again, I stress that description is necessary to make the place come alive for those of us who have never been there. Here are two examples:

El telescopio

Tengo dos telescopios que son
mis ojos para mirarte a ti,
República Dominicana,
Tienes cintura y belleza
y sonrisa del sol inmenso.
En la playa se mira una alegría
rica, pero en el campo
se ve una pobreza intensa.
En mi corazón hay una tristeza,
Quisiera verte de cerca
con mi telescopio infantil,
Mirar los ratoncitos callados
comiendo las frutas de ti,
pequeño país.

—*Charles Mirabal, eighth grade*

The Telescope

I have two telescopes which are
my eyes to look at you,
Dominican Republic,
You have a waist, you have beauty
and the smile of the immense sun.
On the beach there is a delicious
joy, but in the countryside,
intense poverty.
In my heart there is a sadness,
I would like to see you up close
with my childhood telescope,
And look at the little silent mice
eating all your fruit,
little country.

Pueblo Colombiano

Pueblo Colombiano que sufres, y no hay
nadie quien se compadesca de ti.
Mi querida Colombia, ya no quiero que sufras,
no quiero que sigas llorando y derramando tanta sangre
de pena y dolor.
Porque algún día llegará el momento en que puedas
cantar y reír como lo estoy haciendo yo.

Pueblo Colombiano, no llores más, porque Dios
es grande y te cubrirá con su manto de amor
Pueblo Colombiano, mi bello país donde yo nací,
en aquella noche me viste nacer.
Pueblo Colombiano, mi bello país, ya no sufras
más, porque algún día llegará el momento
en que puedas cantar y reír como yo.

—*John Bernardo Tabares, seventh grade*

Colombian People

Colombian people, you suffer and there is
no one who takes pity on you.
My beloved Colombia, I don't want you to suffer any more,
I don't want you to keep crying and spilling so much blood
in pain and sorrow.

Because one day a moment will come when you can
sing and laugh as I am doing.

Colombian people, don't cry, because God
is great and will cover you with a robe of love.
Colombian people, my beautiful country where I was born, on that night you
    saw my birth.
Colombian people, my beautiful country, don't suffer
any more, because one day the moment will arrive
when you can sing and laugh like me.

In the remaining few minutes of the period, when the papers are being handed in, I ask who is interested in reading their poem to the class. The volunteers go first. If there's time left, I read as many poems as I can without giving anyone's name, and ask after each if the writer will identify him or herself. In junior high especially, I find students want their poems read, but prefer a mantle of anonymity regarding authorship.

Bibliography

Miguel Hernández and Blas de Otero: Selected Poems, edited by Timothy Baland and Hardie St. Martin. Boston: Beacon Press, 1972.

MARY SUE GALINDO

Inspiring Young Writers with Chicano *Pinto* Poetry

Recently I taught a creative writing class at a community center in one of the economically depressed developments (*colonias*) in south Texas. I worked with teens (ages 13–19), many of whom had never been exposed to Hispanic writers and were not "into" writing. Unlike school teachers, I had no captive audience. It was up to me to hook these teens.

I began my class with the poetry of Chicano *pintos* (persons who have been or are currently in prison), to dispell any preconceived notions students may have had about poets only being scholars and intellectuals who write about life alien to the students' own experiences.

Another stereotype that I hoped to dismiss was the notion that tough guys, cool dudes, and such don't express themselves with pen and paper. Before students can be fully open to poetry and to looking within themselves, it is important for them to feel comfortable with themselves and not to feel threatened about putting their thoughts and feelings down on paper. It turned out that *pinto* poetry was an attention-getter. Few students, if any, have been exposed to the poetry that comes from within the walls of our penal system.

I began with a poem in Spanish entitled "Quizás" by David Muñoz from the Ellis Unit in Huntsville, Texas. My students were bilingual, but they prefer Spanish. Here is the poem:

Quizás

Ya son las doce de la noche
y no me puedo dormir
recordando mi pasado
y pensando en el porvenir

Aquí me encuentro en mi celda
donde vivo yo encerrado

haciendo día por día
en la pinta del estado

Escogí caminos chuecos
sin ponerme yo a pensar
que a esta pinche penitencia
un día fuera a llegar

Comencé desde muy joven
a robar y a disvariar
y en los bailes y cantinas
me gustaba a mi pelear

Mi madrecita, muy firme
siempre, siempre, me decía
deja esos caminos chuecos
no te vaya a pasar un día

Pero, yo caído de risa
muy chingón le contestaba
no se apure madrecita
no me pasará a mi nada

Ahora sí ya me pesa
ahora que ya es muy tarde
me pesa no haber tomado
los consejos de mi madre

Pues, ya ni llorar es bueno
este arroz ya se quemó
quizás y con esta sopa
se me quite lo pendejo

Quizás, quizás . . .

—*David Muñoz*

Perhaps

It is twelve midnight
and I can't fall asleep
remembering my past
thinking about the future

I find myself in a cell
where I live caged

doing time, day by day
in the state pen

I chose crooked paths
without stopping to think
that in this damn penitentiary
I would one day find myself

I began when I was very young
to steal and to stray
and at dances and in bars
I liked to brawl

My dear mother, so firm
always, always telling me
leave those crooked paths
one day you may regret it

But, I stumbling with laughter
feeling Bad Ass would reply
don't worry mother
nothing will happen to me

Now I regret it
now that it's too late
I regret not having taken
my mother's advice

Well, not even tears can help
this is a done deal
perhaps while I stew
I won't be such a fool

Perhaps, perhaps . . .

—*Translated by Mary Sue Galindo*

After reading the poem, I first called attention to its structure and style. This particular poem uses rhyme, a traditional device for Spanish verse. We then went into a discussion of word choice, rhythm, and meter, and the effort and skill this writer displayed. We looked at the author's use of slang (*pinta*—prison), folk sayings (*dichos*), and profanity (*pinche, chingón*). Do these elements enhance the poem? Are they appropriate? What other folk sayings are you familiar with?

I pointed out that this poem was not written in formal Spanish, because that is not part of who the writer is. Muñoz chose to express himself with the vocabulary that is familiar and natural to him.

Our discussion then focused on the poem's theme and the author's autobiographical, introspective approach. This is a good beginning point for writers—getting them to tell their own stories. As with this poem, not all stories have happy endings. Life is that way. Because young people are open to honest and realistic expression, they are open to introspection.

We then concluded our discussion with an exercise. Pen and paper were set aside for the moment. I turned out the lights and asked the students to close their eyes, to look inside themselves, go inside their memories. I asked, "Is there a situation, an event, a decision that you regret? Is there a feat that you are proud of?" I gave them a few minutes to meditate. Then I turned on the lights and asked students to write about their memories.

But how to get started? I reminded them about the folk sayings we discussed and suggested they use one of their own to start off or include in the poem.

Finally, I gave the students several lines they could use to begin their poems. These "starters" included: "This ain't no place to be . . . ," "I knew I was mistaken . . . ," "An endless sky of diamonds . . . ," and "I went cruisin' late one night. . . ." Later, when students have become more confident and comfortable as writers, they do not have to use this crutch.

Orlando let me know from the start that he was not into poetry or writing. He had been invited by the center director to attend my class, but he was not committing himself. When I had made lesson plans, I had envisioned the likes of Orlando coming around. I knew my material had to speak to him, otherwise he would not be back. At the end of this class, he selected the starter from my list "Buscaba esquina yo" ("I looked around for back-up") and wrote about his prized possession, a lowrider bike that he had put together, and how some guys had jumped him and made off with his bike. I could see that he was pouring out his soul into this piece and at the same time he was wanting assurance because he had never written anything like this before.

Following are three poems by students who also responded to Muñoz's poem. Vicente de León's poem, written in Spanish with some attention to sound and meter, begins with one of the starters from my list:

Sin saber lo que hacía

Sin saber lo que hacía
la otra noche
que a las drogas

me metí
con un consejo en mi mente
que de plano lo olvidé
ahora lloro por mi vida
sin saber qué hacer
espero que algun día
conponga mis errores
de aquella noche tan oscura
que mi vida heche a perder
pero ni modo
ya lo hice y el vicio es el que me sostiene
si tú le buscas
sufrirás
porque este juego
sí es mortal
no lo juegues
porque nunca ganarás

    —Vicente de León

Without Knowing What I Was Doing

Without knowing what I was doing
the other night
the drugs scene
got the best of me
ignoring the voice inside my head
that tried to pull me away
now I cry for my life
I don't know what to do
I am hoping someday
to fix the errors
of that dark night
when I threw my life away
but alas
it is done and my habit is what sustains me
if you play
you will suffer
because the game is mortal
don't play
because you will never win

    —Translated by Mary Sue Galindo

Gabriel Bernard wrote about his experiences growing up in Chicago among *cholos* (boys from the hood) and getting involved with drugs. Like Muñoz, he used some street slang (*mota*—marijuana), but chose to write his poem in English. Gabriel's poem also begins with a starter from my list:

This Ain't No Place to Be

I remember my parents telling me
when I used to walk down the streets.

I remember seeing *cholos* around me
smoking *mota* and sniffing cocaine
around the neighborhood.
I remember joining them
and making my life miserable
like theirs
never realizing that I
was doing wrong.

And now I'm losing my life.
I can't even walk down the streets
or go cruising in my Cadillac
because those *cholos* are after me.

Now that I'm going to lose my life
I'm crying for it.
Now I can't take out those memories
that once my parents told me
"This ain't no place to be."

    —Gabriel Bernard

Esto no es buena onda

Recuerdo que mis padres me decían
cuando caminaba por las calles.

Recuerdo ver cholos alrededor
fumando mota y sorbiendo la cocaina
en mi barrio.
Recuerdo que yo los acompañaba
hechando mi vida a perder
como la de ellos
nunca realizando que
estaba en el mal.

Y ahora estoy perdiendo mi vida.
Ni siquiera puedo caminar por las calles
o dar la vuelta en mi Cadillac
porque esos cholos me persiguen.

Ahora que voy a perder mi vida
lloro por ella.
Ahora no puedo desboraller esas memorias
que alguna vez mis padres me dijeron
"Esto no es buena onda."

—Translated by Mary Sue Galindo

Focusing on the idea of being incarcerated ("encerrada siempre / en la obscuridad / con tanta soledad"), Claudia beautifully expresses her loneliness, frustration, and hope:

La flor

Siempre he sido como una
flor
sin agua y sin luz
encerrada siempre
en la obscuridad
con tanta soledad.

Me siento extraña
con la gente que me mira
y me mira
sin entender mi
sufrimiento.

Pero algun día
me despertaré y sentiré
que nada ha pasado.
La vida me espera.
Necesito levantarme
para volver a ser
aquella flor
que un día estuvo
en aquel jardín
con ese color rojo
tan bello y
tan apasionado.

Mi jardín,
un día
volverá a ti.

The Flower

I've always been like a
flower
without water and light
shut away forever
in darkness
with so much loneliness.

I feel strange
with the people who see me
and they see through me
without understanding my
suffering.

But one day
I will awaken and feel
as though nothing has happened.
Life awaits me.
I need to rise
in order to again become
that flower
that one day thrived
in that garden
with that shade of red
so beautiful and
so passionate.

Beloved garden
one day
I will return.

—Translated by Mary Sue Galindo

Bibliographical Note

David Muñoz's poem was published in *Tonantzin*, a tabloid published by
the Guadalupe Cultural Arts Center, San Antonio, Texas, in the March
1985 issue.

DEBORAH CUMMINS

Questions We Didn't Know We Wanted to Ask
Using Neruda

The teachers who early in my life stood out—who made a difference in how I felt about school, about learning, about myself—have at least one thing in common: they were questioners. They asked questions of us—as individuals, as a class, as a part of a greater world beyond the classroom walls. In the margins of the papers and reports they returned to us were not just checkmarks or terse comments, but more questions asking us to go deeper, consider another angle or viewpoint—prodding at, through questions, our laziness or inattentiveness. Standing at the blackboard or lectern, the best teachers not only offered us precise facts, they dangled before us speculation, even wonder. And, as if the question marks had been sharp and inverted, I was hooked.

But questions, it seems to me, now have fallen out of favor. At all levels, there is an absence of essential, meaningful questioning. For our politicians in debate, questions are scripted from preconceived answers. In literature classes, we learn to ask questions for which there is only one correct answer: "What does Hawthorne's Minister Hooper wear over his face?" rather than "How could such a veil change him into 'something awful, only by hiding his face'?" Today, the question from a child's mouth is too frequently something like "How did he do that?" referring to a special effect in yet another action film.

In my work with young writers, I try to give back some of the kind of questioning that continues to be crucial to my own growth, as a writer and as a person. I introduce (or, in some cases, re-introduce) this notion of questioning and speculation through one of the finest literary models, Pablo Neruda's *Book of Questions* (*El libro de preguntas*), translated by William O'Daly. Here, each poem is a series of questions. The poet asks and, without waiting for or providing answers, moves on to another question, then another, at times sounding like a precocious child who, in the torrent of asking, cares not for responses. As with all Neruda's writing, the world—at its most trivial and its most essential—is his subject, and his language is invested with color and vivid imagery, forming a unique way of looking and asking.

> Why didn't both of us die
> when my infancy died?
>
> Do you hear yellow detonations
> in mid-autumn?
>
> From what does the hummingbird dangle
> its glittering symmetry?
>
> Is 4 always 4 for everybody?
> Are all 7s equal?
>
> What's the name of the flower
> that flies from bird to bird?

I have used Pablo Neruda's question poems in grades 5 through 12, in ESL, bilingual, and all-English-speaking classrooms. Recently, I used them as an introductory first session with a fifth grade class. It was a Monday and I related how I'd been to a weekend family gathering where a lot of small children were present. I'd forgotten, I told them, how at a certain age children ask so many questions. How many of them, I asked, had younger brothers and sisters? And did they ever notice how their siblings asked a lot of questions? In response, eyes rolled, heads nodded enthusiastically. (Students, I've learned, are very interested in knowing about our lives outside the classroom, who we are "unofficially.") Why do you think, I asked my students, that small children ask so many questions? "To find out stuff." "They don't know anything." From across the classroom: "They don't know any better." Yes, I admitted, it is a way of learning, of finding out about the world. But as we get older, I proposed, do you think we tend to ask fewer questions? Silence, then some nods of heads, some "yeahs." Why? "We know everything," someone threw out, getting the laughs. "We're supposed to know." What? You're supposed to know everything? "No, but lots of stuff." "We're afraid to ask," from the back of the room. In the corner, "We don't want to look dumb." Oh, so if we're going to ask questions, it's better to keep them to ourselves. Is it dumb then to wonder aloud in the cafeteria line what you're going to have for lunch—nachos or burgers? "Yeah." Is it dumb to wonder aloud what you're doing on this planet? What you might do with your life that's different than the person sitting next to you? Different than anything anyone's ever done before?

Prompted by my suggestions and observations, posed in almost all cases as questions, a lively discussion followed. (I attempt to divide most of my classroom time as one third presentation/discussion, one third writing, one third reading/sharing. For this lesson, I've learned that sometimes the discussion takes longer.) Some of the points explored during our discussion included:

What's more important: the answer or the question?
What's more powerful?
Do all questions have answers?
Do all questions have only one right answer?
How do we make discoveries about the world?
How do we find out about one another? (I ask students, don't they want to fall in love with someone some day, maybe have a relationship? Needless to say, the difference in response between a fifth grade class and high school is vast!)
Do we all ask the same questions?
Do we all ask questions in the same way?

By way of these last two points, I attempt to direct students' attention to how each of us has a perspective, a particular point of view, wholly our own. The questions we ask and the way in which we ask them say much about who we are. As writers, we call it, in addition to our point of view, our stance on life.

Next, I introduce Neruda's book. I read excerpts aloud, choosing questions I think the students will find most interesting and engaging. (As with all the literary models I use, I try not to let vocabulary stand in my way. If necessary, I'll list a few words on the board, providing brief definitions.) In ESL or bilingual classes, I read the excerpts in both Spanish and English, as we sometimes do in all-English-speaking high school classrooms where students have studied Spanish. In either language, it is impossible to miss Neruda's distinctive use and love of language, his arresting images, his way of asking the questions. Some lines I use include:

Why do the leaves kill themselves
as soon as they feel yellow?

What did the tree learn of the earth
to confide to the sky?

At whom is the rice grinning
with its infinite white teeth?

When prisoners think of the light
is it the same that lights up your world?

Have you wondered what color
April is to the sick?

Who's the magnolia kidding
with its lemon's aroma?

In the sky over Colombia
is there a collector of clouds?

Why does the rain weep with joy,
with or without cause?

How do the seasons discover
it's time to change shirts?

Though I inevitably get in response at least one "weird" and some giggles, Neruda almost always captures the class' attention. I ask the students to notice the questions' vast subject matter and the interesting and surprising ways Neruda has of asking the questions—for example, his playful tone and vivid imagery, his variety of sentence structure, his use of contrast, of personification, and of metaphor (for those classes where this has already been introduced).

Then I go to a student model. What other young writers have written in response to the same literary model can be extremely useful. While there may be some copying or close imitating, hearing exemplary work of their peers can encourage and inspire students. With this fifth grade group, I read some lines from a list poem called "Questions," a class collaboration by eighth graders at the Awty International School in Houston, Texas:

Why is sadness always pushing like a runner to overtake happiness?
Who decided "opposites attract"?
Why does crying help you smile?
Why do clouds move away from me?
Do I see the same moon that people in China see?
Why do people judge each other by their actions when their thoughts might be more harmful?
Does anger make everyone feel like they're on fire?
Why is depression made out of salt water?

Why can't Monday be Wednesday or Sunday?
Why is ignorance so embarrassing?
Is pine-scented insecticide a good idea?
If our arm falls off during life, is it waiting for us in heaven?
Who decided to call this Earth?
Who came up with figurative speech?
Why are certain things inappropriate, and who decided?
How is it that there are more questions than there are answers?

Then students write their own lists of questions. I encourage them to be playful with language and subject matter, like Neruda. Nothing, I tell them, is exempt from wonder. Think back to the cafeteria line, the nachos versus burgers. What question might Neruda find in this? I urge students to free themselves from premature editing (the list format is good for avoiding this). Let your mind roam, I tell them. Consider the world with different, wondering eyes. Ask the questions you always or never knew you wanted to ask.

One virtue of this assignment is that no one can fail. Everyone has questions. Naturally, there will be the class clown, going not for the playful but the silly or the bizarre in order to win the laughs. And there will be those students who only come up with the obvious questions, ones that can be answered with a simple (and obvious) yes or no. But, with most students, I've seen how after an initial warm up, there is a loosening as they become more emboldened, how they fall into an almost rhythmic letting go.

During writing time, I walk around the classroom, encouraging, commenting, suggesting, helping to unstick the stuck. When appropriate, and with the authors' permission, I read aloud good examples. The best results come from hearing a fellow student's writing. The effect is often energizing. For the students who, after four or five queries, think they have exhausted their reservoir of unasked questions, I suggest they go back and look at what they have. Is there another way they might ask their questions, a more vivid word or image they might add?

Then, if time permits, I go around the room and ask for volunteers to read their work aloud. In this fifth grade class, because so many students wanted to read and our time was limited, I asked them to pick their two favorite questions and read them. This is my favorite part, where a certain magic, a wondering, takes over the classroom. In a climate where no question is deemed stupid or too trivial, where all questions are honored, so are our students' ideas, thoughts, hopes and fears. As they admire the work of their fellow writers, they may also learn that someone else's thoughts and anxieties mirror their own and a certain trust and empathy is established.

With this fifth grade class, I collected the students' papers and, at home, put together a class poem. (Depending on the number of students and the quality of the work, I try whenever I assemble a class poem to take at least one line or image from each student.) Then I typed it up. (Seeing their work typed up enables students to get a truer sense of being a writer, particularly in schools were computers are scarce. For some of my students, it's the first time they've ever seen their work "in print.")

I brought the class poem to my next session. To enthusiastic response, I read it then posted it on the board. I also made certain that the school principal received a copy. Here then, from the Greenbriar School in Northbrook, Illinois, is the class collaborative poem:

We Were Wondering . . .

Why are rainy days called gloomy?
Does rain fall because God cries when a young person dies for no reason at
all?
Why do flowers always bloom out and not in?
Does winter always have to come before spring?
How come people say the moon is made of cheese and not waffles, for ex-
ample?
When someone tickles you, why do you laugh?
Why does anger feel like you are under a heavy weight?
Why do things we don't know about scare us?
Why do we make mistakes?
Why did it take so long to discover the light bulb?
Why are there choices that are complicated to some people and not hard to
others?
How come girls have long hair and boys don't?
How come there are more girls than boys in the world?
Why do you see the word "men" in writing every day and not "women?"
Why do people have eyebrows?
Why do we get taller when we get older?
Why do dogs chase cats?
Does every living thing have a way of communicating?
Where does Jimmy Buffet get his songs?
Why is a piece of paper not as valuable as a dollar bill which is also a piece of
paper?
Why do cookies disappear fastest when you're not the one eating them?
How come cake is served at parties?

Why does everything have a name?
Where does time come from?
Are you in complete control of your life or does fate just give you paths?
Is there a limit to everything?
Is anything perfect? Anyone?
What happens if heaven gets too full? Will people get longer lives or will heaven be expanded?
How old is God?
When God created the earth, did he want it to have so many problems?
Do you have to eat and sleep in heaven?
I am what I am, am I anything more?
Is life a play and the ending already made up?

By our asking questions, we keep the curious, eager child alive in all of us. Neruda asks:

Where is the child that I was—
inside of me still—or gone?

For that question, we have the answer.

Note

Some of my work done with Neruda's *Book of Questions* was inspired by former colleagues Mary Pettice and Robin Reagler at Writers in the Schools in Houston, Texas.

Bibliography

Pablo Neruda. *The Book of Questions.* Translated by William O'Daly. Port Townsend, Wash.: Copper Canyon, 1991.

ROSEMARIE ROQUÉ

Talking to Lorca's Moon

"Talking to the Moon" is an exercise for third, fourth, and fifth grade students that I've had some very good results with, and one that uses a character from Spanish folklore and music from Spain. This exercise involves having students write letters to the moon, but it differs from other letter-writing exercises in that the character to whom the children write ("la Luna") is an unusual, fairy tale amalgam of benevolence and indifference, one who has power to make wishes come true but who also has a mysterious mean streak. Using music sets a mood, and the students that I worked with seemed inspired by it.

As a child, I remember listening to my parent's records of music from Spain. One that I especially loved was a recording of poems in Spanish, spoken with great feeling and accompanied by the guitar.[1] Occasionally, the narrator would sing a kind of wailing song ("Cante jondo"), which is sung primarily in Andalusia.[2] It is difficult to describe this type of singing, except to say that it seems to well up from a place of longing and sadness in the singer.

Federico García Lorca's poem "Romance de la luna, luna" is one of the poems recited on this record, and one of the poems before which the narrator plays the guitar and sings his wailing song for a bit. This wailing certainly gets one's attention, and because I thought that it might work well with a writing project, I bought a tape recording of it to class.

What I did with the fourth graders that I was teaching was to start the class by talking about la Luna and her role in the poem. In Lorca's poem, la Luna is a strange, ethereal woman who steals a young boy away from Gypsies. She is cruel in the poem (the child dies), but la Luna can also be a source of good things. She's a force to be contended with, certainly, and respected, but sometimes la Luna can be reasoned with. In our class discussion, I created a fairy tale Luna who was not strictly la Luna from Lorca's poem, but was slightly more benevolent. I emphasized la Luna's good nature, and the fact that she could sometimes be persuaded to do good deeds.

Before playing the tape, I brought up the idea that one character, la Luna, could possess seemingly contradictory motives and desires. It is interesting to hear what fourth graders had to say about the possibility of one person expressing many different—and at times, inconsistent—personality traits.

Then I told the class that we were going to hear the singer speaking to la Luna. The tape itself lasted for only a minute or two. When I stopped the tape, the students were giggly and amused, some of them even imitating the wailing "Cante jondo" sounds that the singer had made (these were fourth graders, remember).

We talked about what the singer must've been saying to la Luna. The class consensus was that he was sad and in desperation. I talked a little bit about what the singer on the tape might have been sad about; I mentioned that la Luna was planning to take a little boy away with her.

At this point, the poem "Romance de la luna, luna" can be read aloud, in Spanish, in the English translation, or both. It should be noted that some of the words need to be defined beforehand, although many students will appreciate the poem's music even if they don't understand every word.

Another note: reading the poem and allowing for some discussion may take up too much class time, especially if you're working within a fifty-minute period. If you're short on time, you might want to read the poem in only one language. Here is Lorca's poem:

Romance de la luna, luna

La luna vino a la fragua
con su polisón de nardos.
El niño la mira, mira.
El niño la está mirando.
En el aire conmovido
mueve la luna sus brazos
y enseña, lúbrica y pura,
sus senos de duro estaño.
—Huye luna, luna, luna.
Si vinieran los gitanos
harían con tu corazón
collares y anillos blancos.
—Niño, déjame que baile.
Cuando vengan los gitanos,
te encontrarán sobre el yunque
con los ojillos cerrados.

—Huye luna, luna, luna,
que ya siento sus caballos.
—Niño, déjame, no pises
mi blancor almidonado.
El jinete se acercaba
tocando el tambor del llano.
Dentro de la fragua el niño
tiene los ojos cerrados.

Por el olivar venían,
bronce y sueño, los gitanos.
Las cabezas levantadas
y los ojos entornados.

Cómo canta la zumaya,
¡ay, cómo canta en el árbol!
Por el cielo va la luna
con un niño de la mano.

Dentro la fragua lloran
dando gritos, los gitanos.
El aire la vela, vela.
El aire la está velando.[3]

Ballad of Luna, Luna

The moon came to the forge
with her petticoat of spikenard.
The boy looks and looks at her.
The boy is looking at her.
In the whirling air
the moon moves her arms
and shows off, slick and pure,
her breasts of hard tin.
—Run luna, luna, luna.
If the Gypsies should come
they'd make of your heart
necklaces and white rings.
—Child, let me dance.
When the Gypsies come
they'll find you over the anvil
with your eyelids closed.
—Run luna, luna, luna,

for now I can hear their horses.
—Child, let me alone. Don't stamp
on my starched whiteness.

The rider came closer,
playing on the drum of the plain.
Inside the forge, the boy
has his eyes closed.

Through the olive grove,
bronze and dreaming, came the Gypsies.
Their heads upraised
and their eyes half-closed.

How the tawny owl sings,
oh, how it sings in the tree!
Through the sky goes the moon
with a boy by the hand.

Inside the forge the Gypsies
cry, letting out shrieks.
The wind is watching, watching it.
The wind is watching over it.

—Translated by William Bryant Logan[4]

For our writing project, I used the format that I always use (and one that students are comfortable with): the collaborative blackboard poem. After we had discussed la Luna and the students had come up with their own ideas from the music and poem, we set out to write a collaborative letter to la Luna. I wrote "Luna, Luna" in large letters on the blackboard, and asked students what we should say to her. The classes with whom I used this project were all lively and creative and had no trouble coming up with imaginative questions to ask the moon, or ways to cajole her, or to scold her for "being mean to people."

My policy during collaborative poems is simple: I write down whatever the kids propose. I try to get the quieter students to volunteer something, and I occasionally shorten things so that everything will fit on the blackboard. I also discourage the shouting out of ideas (who can work when everyone's talking at once?), but aside from this, every line offered gets included. I do this because I think that it makes the whole process of writing seem less threatening. Initially students will suggest only those ideas that they think the teacher will like. In order to upset this routine, I present myself as a teacher who likes everything, and the more outlandish, the better. Once the students realize that I'm not fishing for the right answer, they're often willing to be wonderfully creative and spontaneous.

After writing at least one collaborative blackboard poem and having a student read it aloud, I give the students worksheets. The worksheet is basically a blank sheet with a few words printed on the top and a lot of lines beneath. For whatever reason, many students seem stymied when asked to write on a sheet of loose-leaf. Maybe worksheets are easier to work with because they give the student a finite amount of space on which to write, and because they include some brief instructions: What would you ask la Luna if you could talk to her, and what would she say in response? A few spaces down from this appear the words "Luna, Luna," as I'd written on the board. These words were followed by five or six blank lines (on which the students could write). A second part opens with "And la Luna says . . .," also followed by blank lines.

I taught this lesson in English to students who understood Spanish; they eagerly cried out "the moon!" when I said "la Luna." The point of the lesson was to introduce students to a little snippet of music and a character from Spanish folklore, and also to create a context in which students could wish their wildest dreams as well as discuss their fears. Speaking to la Luna is like wishing on a star, except that la Luna has human qualities and some capriciously cruel ways. This exercise also works well for native speakers of Spanish. Those students that I've taught have always been very receptive to poetry and music written in Spanish, even if it is not from their native country.

This assignment hinges on the concept of a magical Luna. If the concept of la Luna's powers and her vacillation between good and evil isn't made clear, the project becomes a rather straightforward letter writing exercise.

Following are samples of letter-poems written by fourth graders at P.S. 176 in Queens, New York, a few years ago. (The words in italics were either printed on the worksheet or were written by me as I worked individually with the students.)

Luna, Luna,
How do you make yourself light
Why do you have to kill people, you could
just punish them
Could you come down to Earth
Discover the things you can't

see way up there in the sky like the kind
of people there are.

La Luna would say:
I use the stars to lighten
up my appearance and I kill people only
because they do something really bad or
if they kill another person. Sometimes I
might go crazy and kill for no reason. And
I would like to come down to Earth and
discover, because I see and hear things that
I like, like television and music.

    —*Justin M.*

Luna, Luna, I think
of you and your country, and
What I am thinking about, and
can I stay with you, Luna.

She would reply:
You are friendly.
I know moons don't talk, as
I am a magic moon I am the only moon
that can talk. I know I am friendly.
I can't come down from the sky
I don't have legs and arms and I can't walk.

    —*Angela W.*

La Luna says:
"Toys would start to grow on trees!
Today is the last day of school!"
I wish we got out of school at 12:00
I wish I could get a better lock on my new
room so that no one could pick the lock.
I wish I had a brother.

    —*Daisha M.*

I would say:
You shine as bright as a brand new light bulb.
How I feel when I am angry with my mom.
Here I am, now let's talk!

La Luna would say:
"Thank you for telling me that you love
my brightness, and I'm sorry that you're angry with your
mom, but don't tell me your feelings about the argument,
tell her." And that after my visit she will want to come
down for moon cookies and moon tea, but that she can only stay for the
morning. And that she wants to make people believe she is not evil or mean,
yes she is mysterious and good and "*sometimes* bad, it depends what mood I'm
in!"

—*Nakesha A.*

Notes

1. The record is *Versos gitanos* by Miguel Herrero, made by Discos Gema in
Cuba.

2. Cante jondo is part of the tradition of Andalusian music and dance that
also includes flamenco. Like flamenco, cante jondo is energetic and passionate.

3. From *Antología poética* by Federico García Lorca. Selected by Guillermo
de Torre and Rafael Alberti (Buenos Aires: Editorial Losada, 1957).

4. In *Sleeping on the Wing* by Kenneth Koch and Kate Farrell (New York:
Vintage Books, 1981).

Suzann Steele Saltzman

Writing Vignettes with Sandra Cisneros's *House on Mango Street*

I teach at a college preparatory school where there are two Senior English classes: Advanced Placement (AP) English and Senior English. I teach Senior English. My students include a small group who are "AP material," but who for one reason or another chose not to take AP English. Most of the other students have "learning differences": Attention Deficit Disorder (ADD) and dyslexia abound. As we approached the fifth six-weeks, I realized my students' writing was becoming stagnant. They had just finished Research Papers and I wanted to have them write things they wanted to say, not write just to meet my expectations.

Early in the school year, when they looked over the books we would read, the students commented that Sandra Cisneros's *House on Mango Street* looked "short and easy." Since then, they had asked again and again, "When are we going to read *Mango Street*?" Finally the time was upon us. My goal was not only to instill a sense of Latin-American culture as portrayed in the novel, but also to help my students understand Cisneros's writing process.

The House on Mango Street consists of a series of vignettes. Each vignette has its own title and details from the life of Esperanza, a young Latina who tells us about her life and culture.

First we read the introduction, and I had the students highlight one part: "I didn't want to sound like my classmates; I didn't want to keep imitating the writers I had been reading. Their voices were right for them but not for me." We read on and learned that through the process of applying different "voices" from her childhood and youth, Cisneros felt she "found something positive" in her own voice. My students were intrigued with the idea of writing with the voice they use when sitting in the kitchen, say, or the voice they used when they were five. I compared Esperanza's

101

growth to theirs, and it was through Esperanza's changes and different ways of expressing herself that my students began to recognize their own.

Once I was able to get my students to remember the way they expressed themselves when they were younger, they began to realize how they have changed and grown. They also began to understand how people can view the world with different eyes. (This lead to a breakthrough in discussing different cultures and accepting those that are different from one's own.) I was surprised at their enthusiasm when they realized they could now attempt to identify their own different ways of using words at different times in their lives. It was a new freedom, and suddenly they had so much to say.

I worked out a daily routine rather quickly. First, I read the day's vignettes (sometimes only one, sometimes up to three). Next, we discussed four things about them:

1) What images in this vignette evoke her culture? How accurate is the representation?
2) What are the many topics in the vignette?
3) What are some examples of Esperanza's using her own voice?
4) What experiences of your own could you write about?

Each question inspired a list of answers, which I wrote on the board. When we finished the discussion, I wrote the daily writing topic on the board. For instance, after we read and discussed the first vignette, "The House on Mango Street," I wrote "The House on (fill in your own) Street" as the writing topic. During the rest of the class period, the students wrote a vignette with that title or with another title based on our lists on the board.

The following day, before we read the next Cisneros vignettes, I explained to the class that vignette writing would be a daily activity. They would be writing vignettes (one or more) in a notebook, and would revise and develop one vignette to be read aloud to the class and turned in for a grade each Friday. There were only a few complaints about this. We continued with the routine of reading, discussing, topic searching, and writing every day until Friday.

On Friday morning, a student stopped by my room and said, "I can't wait to read my vignette today, you're going to love it." Everyone was prepared for class. The vignettes were beautifully typed and the authors read them aloud with enthusiasm. The students listened intently to each other, and as soon as one completed reading, another raced to the front of the room to read his or her own.

Over the next few weeks, as well as discussing the Cisneros book and its cultural setting, we talked about our personal approaches to writing. Two things convinced me to continue using this lesson plan with future classes. The first was the students' enthusiasm and the accountability of Fridays. The second was the reaction of the other English students, the ones in AP. One day, I saw the AP students in a huddle outside my door. Finally, a chosen representative approached me and told me that their teacher was absent. Could they sit in on my class and listen to the vignettes? I said yes. My own students were happy to have a larger audience, but were noticeably nervous about having to read in front of the more "advanced" students. Nevertheless, they persevered and read what I felt were meaningful, well-written essays. The audience looked awestruck. Later, on two separate occasions, AP students stopped in and said they wished they had a chance "to write that way." One said, "All we ever do is critical analysis. We don't get a chance to use our own voice." One girl said that before they were seniors, this class had not been divided between two different English classes. They had been somewhat familiar with each other's capabilities for years. She said she couldn't believe how great my students were writing now.

As time progressed, the students began to develop their own topics instead of writing to mine.

I divided the vignettes in *The House on Mango Street* as follows:

Vignette	*Suggested writing topic*
1. The House on Mango Street	1. The House on (fill in your own) Street
2. Hairs Boys & Girls	2. Either Symbols Represent Everything or My Toy Represented Me
3. My Name	3. What's in a Name?
4. Cathy Queen of Cat Our Good Day Laughter	4. Only My Friend until. . . Our Good Day Laughter

5. Gil's Furniture Bought & Sold
   Meme Ortiz
   Other Cousin Marin

5. A Character in and out of My
   Life

6. Those Who Don't
   There Was an Old Woman
   Had So Many Children
   She Didn't Know What to Do

6. "They are without respect
   for all living things including
   themselves"

7. Alicia Who Sees Mice
   Darius and the Clouds
   And Some More
   The Family of Little Feet

7. The Crazies

8. A Rice Sandwich
   Hips

8. Tales from School AND
   on the Subject of the
   Opposite Gender

9. The First Job

9. The First Job

10. Papa Who Wakes Up
    Tired in the Dark
    Born Bad

10. Born (fill in the blank)
    and describe how you
    were born

11. Elenita, Cards, Palm, Water
    Geraldo No Last Name
    Edna's Ruthie
    The Earl Of Tennessee

11. It Takes All Kinds to
    Make Up a World

12. Sire
    Four Skinny Trees

12. Scary Stories of Personal
    Experiences

13. No Speak English

13. Write about your day
    today. Explain what
    would have happened if,
    when you awoke, you
    no longer spoke or
    understood English.

14. Rafaela Who Drinks Coconut
    & Papaya Juice on Tuesdays
    Sally
    Minerva Who Writes Poems

14. Love Is Restrictive

15. Bums in The Attic Beautiful & Cruel	15. "But I have decided not to grow up tame like the others who lay their necks on the threshold waiting for the ball and chain."
16. A Smart Cookie What Sally Said The Monkey Garden	16. I Could Have Been Somebody
17. Red Clowns, Linoleum Roses The Three Sisters	17. "You can't erase what you know, you can't erase who you are."
18. Alicia & I Talking on Edna's Steps	18. You and I
19. A House of My Own	19. A House of My Own
20. Mango Says Goodbye Sometimes	20. I Say Goodbye Sometimes

Eventually, we got away from calling our pieces "vignettes," and wrote prose poems, essays, and short stories. Occasionally, I broke with the traditional routine and had them contrast different cultures and analyze the ways these cultures are represented. Often the culture studies inspired some intense conversations over shared (or differing) beliefs, and this led to impassioned writing. Also, I had the students volunteer to read Cisneros's vignettes and lead class discussions.

As well as developing, revising, and presenting one piece of writing each week, the students had to keep their vignette notebooks updated for periodical "notebook checks," and they had to turn the notebooks in for a journal grade at the end of the six-week grading period. I noticed that my students took special care with organization and keeping private writing "private." Many of them carried around their vignette notebooks so protectively that it seemed as if their own voices really *were* treasured therein.

The Cisneros vignette "Our Good Day" begins, "If you give me five dollars I will be your friend forever." I use this childish statement as a way to help students jump back to a time when they said or heard such things. Many of them recalled "I won't be your friend anymore if you don't. . . ." Suddenly we're back in first grade—everyone had an experience they recalled. Once Friday rolled around and everyone read aloud, I had the audience note statements that captured a younger voice. Often I wrote these statements on the board and we discussed how the voice in them sounded different from the voice the writer usually uses.

Other times we focused more on the writer's feelings. After discussing the feeling of "friendship bribery," Evan D. wrote about an experience of beginning to feel accepted:

> The only kids living near me are older. They don't like me and I can never play with them. One day two guys down the street decide they will let me play music at their pretend-concert. Wowwy, I can't wait. All I do is bring my tape and press the play button on the stereo. It made me feel so 100% special that I can still remember the feeling.

One student's willingness to be open always gives the others courage. Once the students start opening up, their trust in each other deepens and they become more willing to be honest in their writing. Not only do the students discover and add voice to the feelings they have about their own experiences, they also begin to gather details to delineate characters in their own writing. They learn through creating fiction that they are able to make sense of experiences and to communicate what they learn from those experiences.

One lesson that Esperanza learned is that there are "bad" people in the world. Almost all my students have a memory of a similar realization. In "The Family of Little Feet," Cisneros describes the feeling of maturity and freedom Esperanza and her friends feel when they first walk in high heels. They feel they are Cinderella until a "bad" man begins to give them the creeps:

> Bum man is yelling something to the air but by now we are running fast and far away, our high heel shoes taking us all the way down the avenue and around the block, past the ugly cousins, past Mr. Benny's, up Mango Street, the back way, just in case. (Cisneros, 42)

This vignette inspired one of my students, Lauren, to recall a time when she was frightened that her grandfather might be considered a bad man:

> School is out for today and I am playing with my friends on the playground. I turn around and see Pop-pop standing on the other side of the fence. I forget about my friends and race to see him. He picks me up with his big arms and a smile and lifts me over the fence. I look and see his smile disappear. Some of the teachers are new at my school and they do not know Pop-pop. They look nervous to me when they are asking me if I know who this man is. Why do they not want me to go with him? Is he a bad man? I am confused because I do not know why my teachers are asking me these things. Pop-pop seems mad at the teachers. After he explains everything to them, we get in his truck and sing songs all the way to his house. When we get there he lets me eat ice cream and drink buttermilk like every other day after school.

Some of the experiences recalled in the students' writing were very painful. When memories were too embarrassing or painful to share, I explained that the authors can always say that they have added a lot of fictional details to make the writing more vivid. That way, the reader will not know for sure which detail is fact and which is fiction, making the writer feel safer.

Throughout *The House on Mango Street*, Cisneros describes Esperanza's feelings about the members of her family. In many ways it is these passages that have inspired some of the best writing from my students. Many of them live in families of step-parents and step-siblings, and many harbor resentment toward their parents because of childhood experiences. I remind my high school seniors that at some point soon they will have to stop blaming their parents and be accountable for their own actions and decisions.

Over time, Esperanza is able to accept her family's plight and herself. For her this is a hard lesson, one that inspires my students. In the vignette, "Papa Who Wakes Up Tired in the Dark," Esperanza recognizes her father's human side. She describes his reaction to his father's death.

> My Papa, his thick hand and thick shoes, who wakes up tired in the dark, who combs his hair with water, drinks his coffee, and is gone before we wake, today is sitting on my bed.
>
> And I think if my own Papa died what would I do? I hold my Papa in my arms. I hold and hold and hold. (Cisneros, 57)

Seeing the human side of one's parents is almost impossible at age seventeen or eighteen. In some of my students' writing I have seen a glimmer of this realization, while in others' I have observed a sudden maturity and change of attitude. One of my seniors, Dan, apparently self-sufficient, wrote about a realization and a need:

> The situation is a "Catch-22." If my father stops criticizing my efforts, then I might feel better in the present. However, his criticisms, although painful, help me to be strong in the long run. It must be hard to have to decide between soothing your son's pain or making him into a strong, self-efficient human being. I know that my father is an extremely intelligent man, and I trust his decision making abilities. I am glad he has made me so strong by his callous behavior, but sometimes I wish that he would care a little more, and show it.

Near the end of the unit, I handed out a questionnaire. To one question, Charlotte responded:

I believe I have found my voice because I don't think "what does the teacher want me to write and how would they phrase this, etc. . . ." I just write creating my own picture, visualizing the scene and putting it into words. I feel comfortable with the way I write. It's almost like a snowflake—no two people write the same—that is if they write in their own voice.

Although most students felt that the results of "finding their own voices" were a success, some felt that although the project was fun, their analytical form of writing really didn't change. Some had difficulty breaking with traditional essay forms, and they were uncomfortable writing in the first person. Most agreed the Cisneros unit was a nice beginning for identifying one's style, the uniqueness each person can bring to the page, and all agreed that it's important to see writing as an outlet for self-expression.

I was most pleased with the new awareness the students had of their own strengths as writers and I was happy that the unit had given them an opportunity to show respect and appreciation for one another. In the course of it all, I realized that I had established a new writing relationship with my students. In future class discussions, my opinions and suggestions about their writing were not only more readily accepted, but sought. We closed the school year with the study of poetic forms and devices, and the students asked for suggestions for poetry writing and encouraged me to write with them.

I also noticed that their abilities to "show" were more developed and their confidence in their own opinions, as expressed in their writing, was more obvious. My objective, in sending these seniors to college, is to ensure not only that they know various writing domains, but also that they go with tools they can use to approach writing assignments. Mostly I want them to realize they have something to say, and they have their own important voice they can use to say it.

Esperanza is a good role model for this, because she wrote from her heart, not from a need to sound like everyone else.

Bibliography

Cisneros, Sandra. *The House on Mango Street*. New York: Vintage, 1991.

John Oliver Simon

The Flowered Song
Learning from Aztec & Mexican Poetry

Some years ago, John Oliver Simon and Roberto Bedoya, two poets from Oakland, California, spent a week in Mexico City teaching poetry writing, with local poets, to elementary school children. A few months later, three poets from the Mexican residency (poets Jorge Luján, Juvenal Acosta, and Roberto García Moreno) returned the visit, working with children in Oakland. The program was sponsored by California Poets in the Schools and the National Museum of Anthropology in Mexico City. This is the first such international exchange we know of, and is documented in Un techo del tamaño del mundo / A Roof the Size of the World *(see the bibliography at the end of this essay). In the excerpts below, Simon translated the children's poetry, most of which was written in Spanish.*—Editor

In most classes, we began talking about the concept of Flower and Song, "flor y canto," the *xochitl in cuicatl* of the Aztecs. We pointed out that the Aztec codices show an unadorned word coming out of the mouth of a king or a god to indicate ordinary speech; but when the word that emerges from the mouth is decorated with flowers, that is poetry. "The flowered word" mediated between man and the universe, between the community and the gods. In order to create this *palabra florida*, we must employ the imagination: that faculty within us that makes images, makes pictures, fantasizes, and travels beyond the confines of logic and the classroom. In poetry, we play with words, as if words were as light as petals and feathers, as if what we say has as much meaning as the songs of birds.

Lies to Quetzalcoatl (John Oliver Simon)
In the gallery devoted to the sacred city of Teotihuacan in the Museo Nacional, there is an impressive reconstruction of the Pyramid of Quetzalcoatl, adorned with seashells representing water; the goggle-eyed masks of Tlaloc, god of the rain; and the fierce plumed heads of the Feath-

ered Serpent. These are so huge that you can stick your arm up to the
shoulder in the mouth of the god. Legend has it that if you do so and then
tell a lie, CHOMP! Quetzalcoatl will bite off your arm. The assignment,
then, was to tell lies to Quetzalcoatl—with the ultimate paradox in mind
that a good lie can be more true than the truth.

> Quetzalcoatl, god of water,
> of song and fire.
> His pyramid has a thousand
> heads of birds and water
> issues from those heads,
> at night the moon comes by
> and dances with the sun and
> fifty rabbits play
> a jazz song,
> while some burros
> fire rockets.
>
>   *—Gabriel Gutiérrez García*

> Quetzalcoatl God of water
> lion full of dove's feathers.
> Soul of steel God of the universe
> passionate for love but
> if anyone does something to him
> he is fierce with warrior's blood
> his pyramid full of hearts
> with shells and fish.
>
>   *—Esmerelda Hernández Mendoza*

> I am the god
> of dance and my fangs
> sing, I have tiny fangs
> like hands
> with my yellow mouth
> I say colored words
> and when I fall
> to earth I change
> the words to music
> I look upon music

and dance everywhere
and inside of me
there is dance and music
and men surrender
themselves to me
my secret saying is:
rhythm and horror
give rhythm to the horror.

—*Israel Bautista*

Haiku (Jorge Luján)

In Mexican haiku, the first and third lines usually rhyme. Juan José Tablada, whose home in Coyoacan is preserved as a national shrine, was the best known *haikuista* of Mexico. He wrote:

Tierno saúz
casi oro, casi ambar,
casi luz . . .

Tender willow,
almost gold, almost amber
almost light . . .

Jorge Luján's haiku recipe with fourth graders neither rhymed nor counted syllables:

1. First line: something usual
2. Second line: something that happens quickly, at once
3. Tie them together, wrap it up, what does it all mean, what happens next?

My desk is always messy.
I shut my desk and left.
Then my desk is clean and I'm messy.

—*Lorena García*

The street is dark
people go along the street
and people scare the darkness.

—*José Miranda*

Hymn to the Sun (John Oliver Simon)

On their first day in the National Museum, the children seated themselves in the outdoor auditorium and were greeted with the invitation to write a *bienvenida* (welcome) to the sun. Each child contributed one line, orally, while poet Alberto Blanco acted as the group scribe. After a while Otto-Raúl González suggested we stop saying what the sun does and simply address it: "Hot mass! Giant orange! Balloon of fire covering us with light!" Following up on a previous Neruda/Questions exercise we had done [See Deborah Cummins's essay elsewhere in this volume— *Ed.*], Alberto suggested we ask the sun questions. Finally I noted that we had three handwritten pages and it was time to begin seeking a way to end the poem. What surprised us was how *pre-Columbian* the resulting poem was.

Hymn to the Sun

Hi!
Hi, friend!
How are you?
You who shine
and give us light all morning
and illumine the Mexican earth
—our country—;
you who say goodbye to us
with rays at evening.
Your heat and brilliance
give us joy and enthusiasm
for work.

We can't look at you directly
but we see you in the mind
with the eyes closed.
You who illumine
all the corners of the world,
at evening
you seem to be covered with blood.
You who make us wait
for the fresh morning,
from some places
you let yourself be seen often.
You are really our friend.

And when someone is sick
you make him better the next morning.
You who give the plants light
and make the trees green again,
you who warm
the water of the pool
you truly give us life.
You who make shine
the water of the sea,
you also make the rainbow appear
which feeds us with happiness
every time we see it.

Hot mass!
Giant orange!
Balloon of fire covering us with light!
A giant ball!

Why do you never fall to earth?
Why can't we look at you directly?
Why do you hide every night?
Why can't we see you all day?

Did you ever catch cold
And where do you sleep at night?
Why can't we touch you?
Why don't you ever move?

You who dominate the whole city,
may you never cease to shine,
because for us you are everything;
there is no one like you.

Goodbye religious star!
So long friend of light!
You are a golden dragon
and your shining amazes us.
That is all we can think.
Never cease to be our friend.
Goodbye, comrade of the soul!

Emerge from the Animal (John Oliver Simon)

In every Mesoamerican culture there is a recurrent motif of the god or hero who emerges from the mouth of a beast. Tezcatlipoca, the tempter, comes out of a tiger's mouth (or wears a tiger's skin, revealing only his face); Quetzalcoatl is born out of the jaws of a serpent. A masterpiece of Toltec art shows a bearded warrior coming out of the mouth of a coyote encrusted with abalone and mother-of-pearl. The Aztec eagle knight wears the eagle mask, and the tiger knight is disguised as a jaguar. Kukulcan, at Uxmal, comes out of a snake's jaws, while the anonymous earth goddess of the Huastecas appears in the beak of a parrot. Standing outdoors in the door of the Temple of Chac, outside the Mayan Hall—and thus in the mouth of a monster animal-god of the rain—I gave the assignment: what animal is inside you, what animal comes out of you, or out of what animal do you emerge? The heavens responded: it began to rain as the children wrote their poems.

The Tiger

The tiger is an animal
that only has two lives,
one inside me
and the other in the body of space.

    —*Soledad Funes*

What's inside Me

A while ago I discovered
that I had
a cat inside me
because when they
treat me well I'm
affectionate, understanding,
loving, but when
they mistreat me I
get mad and behave
differently than usual
I behave badly,
I'm dense, difficult,
just
like a rooster, that's why
I said what I had

inside me because
unfortunately today
I discovered that I don't have
anything inside me.

> —*Claudia Uribe García*

Chac

Chac is raining, Chac is crying
raining loosens his sadness, out of an animal,
discharging his fury weeping,
finally, we all came out of an animal

> —*Juan Sosa*

Coyote Knight

It's a man swallowed by the imagination of a Toltec.

> —*Jamsré Torres*

Songs of the Animals (Roberto Bedoya)

Using a model poem written by a fourth grader in California, we asked the children to write about animals, using colors, seasons, and the five senses.

In my heart lives a horse
that horse says to me
come and I'll take you to the country
get up on me and you'll see
how much fun we will have
galloping and jumping.

> —*Azahel Estudillo*

My Hen

My hen
my hen
is mine
is mine
on her little path
on her little path
goes into the night
the hen is mine
the hen is mine

there are lots and lots
there's no other like mine

　　　—*Francisco Morales Rosas*

The Singing Shoes (several poets)

The rhythms of the *lirica infantil* of Mexico are as alive to recent immi-
grant children in the U.S. as Mary-had-a-little-lamb is to standard-culture
Americans. The accents of the *corrido* and *mariachi* are as alive in the inner
ear as the latest rap from the ghetto blaster. And what about the other
rhythms of life, the shoes slapping, the galaxies revolving, red and green
and yellow lights, dusk and dawn, birth and death?

Bark

When the mailman
comes by I hear a
bark when the newspaper
boy comes by I hear
a bark I'm tired of
hearing sounds that go
bark bark bark I'm tired
of it because I'm trying
to sleep when the garbage
man comes the barks get
even louder so I have
to buy a gun and
waste my money and
on every Tuesday I have
to kill the garbage man so I
can sleep. But this goes
on and on. But one day
I might be in jail
for killing the garbage man
but the dogs will still
go bark, bark, bark
and bark.

　　　—*Gilbert Vega*

Little Coyote Coyote

Little coyote coyote
where are you going?

To the hacienda of Saint Nicholas
and there I will
eat a little hen
that you won't give me
and the one that you gave me
I already ate
and the one you will give me
I will eat
how do you like it
fried or roasted?
fried
so heat up the butter
so heat up the butter

　　　—*Guadalupe Jiménez*

Shoes Singing

I went to school
shoes singing rapidly
I went to open the door
shoes singing rapidly
I went to the dance
shoes singing rapidly
I couldn't understand it already and
shoes singing rapidly
I stood out on a mountain
and shoes singing rapidly
I threw them in the garbage
and they sang more rapidly
they said you're getting mad
you're getting mad
you're getting mad

　　　—*Ricardo Ahumada*

Annotated Bibliography

Un techo del tamaño del mundo: A Roof the Size of the World, edited by John Oliver Simon (Oakland, Calif.: Oakland Unified School District, 1987). Documentary of an international poetry-teaching exchange between California Poets in the Schools and the National Museum of Anthropology in Mexico City. Bilingual text with forty writing exercises and hundreds of student poems from Mexico and Oakland. To order, send $10 to John Oliver Simon, 2209 California, Berkeley, CA 94703.

Light from a Nearby Window: Contemporary Mexican Poetry, edited by Juvenal Acosta (San Francisco: City Lights, 1993). Important anthology of twenty Mexican poets born since 1945.

Diccionario de la imaginación, edited by Jorge Luján (Mexico City: Taller Nacimiento, 1986). Jorge Luján independently invented the idea of poetry teaching in a private workshop in Mexico. His students, ranging from seven to twelve years old, have produced superb poems. Spanish text. To order, send international money order for $10.00 to Jorge Luján, Av. Arteaga y Salazar 446, Casa 5, Colonia Contadero Cuajimalpa, Mexico DF, 05500, Mexico.

La Luciérnaga: Antología para niños de la poesía mexicana contemporánea, edited by Francisco Serrano with illustrations by Alberto Blanco (Mexico City: Editorial Cidcli, 1983). A comprehensive and delightful collection of twentieth-century Mexican poetry chosen for children, with magnificent collages by Blanco. Spanish text. This anthology is generally available in better bookshops in Mexico City, and can probably be ordered through Spanish-language distributors such as Bookworks in San Francisco.

In Xochitl in Cuicatl: Flor y Canto: La poesía de los Aztecas by Birgitta Leander (Mexico City: Instituto Nacional Indigenista, SEP, 1972). The "flower and song" poetry of the Aztecs is fundamental to the deep culture of Mexican and Chicano children. Nahuatl texts are available in Spanish and English for the teacher who's willing to hunt through libraries and bookstores. Some pre-Columbian texts are translated (into English) in Jerome Rothenberg's anthologies *Technicians of the Sacred* and *Shaking the Pumpkin.*

Antología de la poesía hispanoamericana, edited by Juan Gustavo Cobo Borda (Mexico City: FCE, 1985); *Antología de la poesía hispanoamericana actual,* edited by Julio Ortega (Mexico City: siglo ventiuno, 1987); and *Poesía Mexicana II: 1915–1979,* edited by Carlos Monsiváis (Mexico City: Promexa Editores, 1979). There is no shortage of excellent anthologies in Spanish of modern Latin American poetry. The North American teacher who wants to use these books in a bilingual classroom must first find the books, and then sort through the poetry to find works that are appropriate and accessible to children. A daunting task.

Poets of Nicaragua 1918–1979: A Bilingual Anthology, translated by Steven F. White (Greensboro, N.C.: Unicorn Press, 1982), and *Poets of Chile 1960–1985: A Bilingual Anthology,* also translated by Steven F. White (Greensboro, N.C.: Unicorn Press, 1986). These excellent anthologies make available the important recent and contemporary poetry of Nicaragua and Chile in facing bilingual format. There are many gems here that can be used in the classroom. Highly recommended.

A Nation of Poets: Writings from the Poetry Workshops of Nicaragua, translated with an introduction by Kent Johnson (Los Angeles: West End Press, 1985); and *Nicaraguan Peasant Poetry from Solentiname,* translated by David Gullette (Los Angeles: West End Press, 1986). Naïve and moving poems by peasants, soldiers, and students, recounting experiences of love and revolution. Bilingual text.

Roots & Wings: Poetry from Spain 1900–75, edited by Hardie St. Martin (New York: Harper & Row, 1976). Bilingual anthology of the great poems from *la patria madre* in this century.

Destruction of the Jaguar: Poems from the Books of Chilam Balam, translated by Christopher Sawyer-Lauçanno (San Francisco: City Lights, 1987). New English edition of lyric passages from one of the great Mayan books.

Volcán: Poems from El Salvador, Guatemala, Nicaragua and Honduras, translated by Alejandro Murguia and Barbara Paschke (San Francisco: City Lights, 1983). Excellent bilingual anthology from Central America. Many poems with a political orientation.

Love Poems from Spain and Spanish America, translated by Perry Highman (San Francisco: City Lights, 1988). Bilingual anthology.

The Renewal of the Vision: Latin American Women Poets 1940–80 (San Francisco: Spectacular Diseases Press, 1987). The poetry establishment in Latin America is heavily male-dominated: a sampling, for instance, of anthologies of Peruvian poetry is ninety-seven percent male! But some good woman poets, such as Blanca Varela in Peru, Rosario Castellanos in Mexico, Claribel Alegria in El Salvador, and Gioconda Belli in Nicaragua, with a host of younger writers, challenge that assumption. Bilingual text.

Cómo formar un taller de creatividad literaria by Edgar Allan García (Fundación Vida Integral, Apartado postal 155-A, 12 de Octubre, Quito, Ecuador, 1993). The author, a young Ecuadorean poet named after Poe, agreed to do a children's workshop at a cultural center in Quito, and found himself reinventing a spontaneous and informal approach to teaching writing. A rich resource of writing exercises.

Arcoiris de sueños: así juegan los niños mexicanos (Nacional Financiera, Mexico City, 1995). A coffeetable book of photographs of antique Mexican toys. Worth the price of admission are the little poems by poet-teacher Jorge Luján that accompany the photos: "In the crystal of one bubble / the whole earth / reflects itself // pop! / another planet gone."

Más de dos siglos de poesía norteamericana. Volume 1 edited by Eva Cruz, volume 2 by Alberto Blanco (Mexico City: Universidad Nacional Autónoma de Mexico, 1993, 1994). Almost 2,000 pages of North American poetry in facing bilingual format, from Anne Bradstreet to Gary Soto and Rita Dove. A handsome boxed edition.

El Libro de la Escritura by Pingüino Tinto (New York: Teachers & Writers, 1989). An expanded, revised translation of T&W's *The Writing Book*, a creative writing workbook for students in grades 3–6, students in elementary Spanish, etc. The only such workbook available in Spanish. Includes many good examples.

CAROL BEARSE

Singing with the Words
Using Neruda and Lorca with Middle School Students

It's the words that sing, they soar and descend.—Pablo Neruda

Like Pablo Neruda, my middle school students have taught me that words sing, helping us to soar when we're happy, or calming us down when we're afraid and confused. As a poet, I apprentice myself under Neruda and Federico García Lorca to enrich my poetry with metaphors and to develop my writing of odes and poems of address.

As a teacher and reading specialist working with adolescents, I depend upon my students to inform my teaching. I have found that by using Neruda and García Lorca's poems in my classroom, I have been able to enhance students' poetry writing in both my bilingual and English classes. I have also found that these poets serve as mirrors for my students by exemplifying the beauty and lyricism of the Spanish language. Here are some of the successful strategies that I have developed.

Namings: A Way to Enrich Metaphors

I often use García Lorca's "Noche" as a model to develop students' sense of metaphor:

Noche

Cirio, candil,
farol y luciérnaga.
La constelación
de la saeta.

Ventanitas de oro
tiemblan,
y en la aurora se mecen
cruces superpuestas.

Cirio, candil,
farol y luciérnaga.

    —Federico García Lorca

Night

Candle, lamp,
lantern and firefly.

The constellation
of the dart.

Little windows of gold
trembling
and cross upon cross,
rocking in the dawn.

Candle, lamp,
lantern and firefly.

    —Translated by Jaime de Angulo

In one bilingual eighth grade class, we first discussed Lorca's unusual names for night, and I encouraged students to think of unusual names for the common things that they saw around them every day, and to think of the qualities of these objects, or the relationship of a particular object to other things near it. We brainstormed aspects of things: color, texture, size, movement, shape, purpose, weight, emotion, relatives, homes. These kinds of lists help students to see the many ways we can look at things by using metaphor. I stress to students that metaphor can make the ordinary extraordinary. For example, the sea could be named the home of whales, the road for ships, the gift of mermaids, or the mirror for clouds. As we went around the room naming things, students began choosing their topics. The following poems are highly evocative:

La luna

La risa de la noche.
La cara que nos mira en la noche.
La novia de la noche.
La prima de las estrellas.

The Moon

The smile of night.
The face that sees us at night.
Night's fiancée.
The stars' cousin.

—*Leonel Núñez, eighth grade*

El cielo

El cielo es un planeta de pajaritos.
El cielo es el río que corre por el pasto.
El cielo es el corazón del mundo.
El cielo es la piel cuadrada de mi madre triste.
El cielo es el corral de los angeles.

The Sky

The sky is a planet of the birds.
The sky is the river that runs through the pasture.
The sky is the heart of the world.
The sky is the skin of my sad mother.
The sky is the angels' yard.

—*Angela Ventura, eighth grade*

El espacio es el corazón de un niño sin el amor de madre.
El espacio es una familia sin un miembro amado.
El espacio es el cielo lleno de estrellas.
El espacio es una noche sin luna.
El espacio es la eternidad de nuestra felicidad.

Space is the heart of a child without its mother's love.
Space is a family missing a loved one.
Space is the sky filled with stars.
Space is night without a moon.
Space is the eternity of our happiness.

—*Rosaura de la Cruz, seventh grade*

I love Rosaura's last line; its abstract simplicity approaches Lorca's. Her first line is an imaginative and startling metaphor.

These exercises in writing metaphor have also helped my students' writing in sixth grade non-bilingual English classes. I provide students with packets of Lorca's poems, which I read aloud, in both Spanish and English, in order to encourage anglophones to appreciate the musicality of the original Spanish. If there are native Spanish speakers in the class, I encourage them to read the Spanish. We also compare Lorca's metaphors with those of writers such as Gary Soto ("Oranges") and Sandra Cisneros ("My Name"). After exploration and discussion, Emma Herrera, a seventh grader, wrote these lines about the sun:

> The sun is a raging ball of fire.
> The sun is the angry goddess of fire.
> The sun is the heat of our mother the earth.
> The sun is the eye of our father the sky.
> The sun is a red and yellow disc.
> The sun is a golden peach growing in the sky.

Ana Pineiro, another seventh grader, was inspired by the wind:

> The wind is a lullaby humming to the earth.
> The wind is a whisper blowing beneath the trees' leaves.
> The wind is a monster scolding us with his anger.
> The wind is a dance partner waltzing with the grass and trees.
> The wind is an instrument playing its own song.
> The wind is a pair of arms hugging the earth in warmth.

Ana's poem illustrates the sophistication of her use of language. Her choice of words contains the inherent musicality of the wind. "Whisper blowing beneath the trees' leaves," "monster scolding us," "dance partner waltzing the grass and trees" are beautiful alliterative combinations.

Playing with Rhythm and Rhyme

I am always on the look-out for Lorca poems that have unusual patterns that we can experiment with. His "Vals en las ramas" inspired me partly because of its formal qualities:

> Cayó una hoja
> y dos
> y tres
> Por la luna nadaba un pez.
> El agua duerme una hora
> y el mar blanco duerme cien.
> La dama
> estaba muerta en la rama.
> La monja

cantaba dentro de la toronja.
La niña
iba por el pino a la piña.
Y el pino
buscaba la plumilla del trino.
Pero el ruiseñor
lloraba sus heridas alrededor.
Y yo también
porque cayó una hoja
y dos
y tres.
Y una cabeza de cristal
y un violín de papel
y la nieve podría con el mundo
una a una
dos a dos
y tres a tres.
¡Oh duro marfil de carnes invisibles!
¡Oh golfo sin hormigas del amanecer!
Con el numen de las ramas,
con el ay de las damas,
con el cro de las ranas,
y el gco amarillo de la miel.
Llegará un torso de sombra
coronado de laurel.
Será el cielo para el viento
duro como una pared
y las ramas desgajadas
se irán bailando con él.
Una a una
alrededor de la luna,
dos a dos
alrededor del sol,
y tres a tres
para que los marfiles se duerman bien.

—*Federico García Lorca*

A leaf fell
and two
and three
while the moon was swimming with a fish
The water sleeps an hour

and the white sea sleeps a hundred.
The lady was dead on the branch.
The nun
sang inside the grapefruit.
The girl
was going for the pine of the pineapple.
And the pine
was looking for the feather of the trill.
But the nightingale
was crying her wounds around.
And I also
because a leaf fell
and two
and three.
And a glass head
and a paper violin
and the snow could hold the world
one by one
two by two
three by three.
Oh, strong ivory of invisible flesh!
Oh, gulf without ants at dawn!
with the poetic inspiration of the branches,
with the pain of the ladies,
with the ribbet of the frogs,
and the yellow earth of honey.
A torso of a shadow will arrive
crowned with the laurel wreath.
The earth will be for the wind
Strong like a wall
and the torn branches
will go dancing with him.
One by one
around the moon,
two by two
around the sun,
and three by three
so that the ivory will sleep well.

— *Translated by Carol Bearse & Esta Montano*

In this poem the falling action of one object causes mysterious things to happen. I asked students in an eighth grade bilingual class to imagine a specific object and think of what series of events could happen as a result of its falling. Looking at the rhyme scheme, we noticed that the rhyming patterns helped to push the poem into another realm. Also, I brought my students some reproductions or works by artists Dalí, Magritte, Kahlo, and De Chirico, who painted images in unusual combinations. The captivating images of my students' poems produced in the classroom a feeling of lightness and a joy in wordplay, as in the following poem by an eighth grader:

Vals a la rosa

Cayó una rosa
y dos
y tres.
Por el viento volaba un cangrejo
y el cielo estaba bien.
La niña
lagrimaba
y yo estaba en la cama;
ella buscaba la luz del cielo
y yo también la buscaba
porque cayó una rosa
y dos
y tres.
Por eso me puse triste y lloré
y una planta de papel
y un caballo comía miel
y la mosca, lo miraba a él.
Una a una
dos a dos
y tres a tres
¡Oh piedra de madera!
¡Oh casa de papel!
con ruido de las abejas,
con el quiquiriquí del gallo,
y el miau del gato.
Llegará una vaca gorda
condenada a morir.
¿Será el viento tan duro
como el huracán?
Andrés irá muriendo con él.
Una a una

como la cumbia
dos a dos
alrededor del balcón
y tres a tres
para que se muevan las paredes.

    —Gissett Genao, eighth grade

Waltz of the Rose

A rose fell
and two
and three
A crab flew in the wind
and the sky was well.
The little girl's eyes
teared
and I was on the bed
she looked for the light of the sky
and I also looked for it
because a rose fell
and two
and three.
Because of this, I became sad and cried
and a plant was made of paper
and a horse ate honey
and the fly looked at him.
One by one
two by two
three by three
Oh, stone made of wood!
Oh, house made of paper!
With the buzz of the bees
with the cockadoodledoo of the rooster
and the meow of the cat.
A fat cow will arrive
condemned to death.
Will the wind be as hard
as the hurricane?
André will go on dying with him.
One by one
just like a *cumbia*
two by two

around the porch
and three by three
so the walls can move.

—*Translated by Carol Bearse & Carmen Dávila*

Gissett's poem is outstanding in the rhyming pattern of the words that she chose, like *papel* (paper), *miel* (honey), and *él* (him). She also used internal near-rhyme in her line "oh piedra de madera" ("oh, stone of wood"). Alas, it's much harder to use rhyme so naturally in English. Gissett, a talented poet, uses startling images to transport us into the surreal. The mood is one of great drama and sadness.

In contrast, both Leonel and Rigoberto wrote their "waltzes" with a playful, almost childlike quality, using the rhyme scheme to build one fanciful event upon the other:

Vals del rayo

Cayó un rayo
y dos
y tres
por encima de la montaña
y acabó con una cama.
La dama
asustada en la cama.
La niña
quitaba
y rezaba
y yo también
porque cayó un rayo
y dos y tres.
Un rayo brillante
una tarde asustante.
El rayo es muy raro
la tierra también
y por eso yo creo que vuelvo a
nacer.
Una a una
bailando en la cuna
dos a dos
cantando nació
tres a tres le vuelvo a temer.

—*Leonel Núñez, eighth grade*

The Waltz of the Ray

A ray fell
and two
and three
on top of the mountain
and it zapped a bed.
The lady
afraid in the bed.
The little girl
screamed
and prayed
and I as well
because a ray fell
and two and three.
A shining ray
a frightening afternoon
The ray is very strange
the earth as well
and because of that I think
I am being born again.
One by one
dancing in the cradle
two by two
singing being born
three by three I am afraid of it again.

—Translated by Carol Bearse & Carmen Davila

Vals en el mar

Cayó una mujer
y dos
y tres.
El sol nadó como un pez.
La dama
estaba muerte en la taza.
La niña
iba por el mar hacia el agua
y el aguacate
buscaba la punta del hoyito.
Yo también
porque cayó una mujer
y dos

y tres
y una cabeza que se besa
y una guitarra de taza
y el hombre podría ser mujer
una a una
dos a dos
y tres a tres.

  —*Rigoberto Vega, eighth grade*

Waltz in the Sea

A woman fell
and two
and three.
The sun swam like a fish
The lady
was dead in a cup.
The little girl
was going along the ocean
towards the water
and the avocado
was looking for the top of
the little hole.
I as well
because one woman
and two
and three
and a head that is kissed
and a guitar of cup
and the man could be a woman
one by one
two by two
and three by three.

  —*Translated by Carol Bearse & Carmen Dávila*

Using Neruda's Stones of the Sky

Stones of the Sky is filled with poems of color; in this case, the color is found in the precious stones of the earth—Neruda cleverly connects his celebrations of color to a greater celebration of man's connection to the earth. I have found that these poems can help adolescents explore color in a very astute way; they also help students use language more precisely by weaving personification into poems of address.

Neruda's poem about turquoise is one of my favorites:

III

Turquesa, te amo como si fueras mi novia,
como si fueras mía:
en todas partes eres:
eres recién lavada,
recién azul celeste:
recién caes del cielo:
eres los ojos del cielo:
rompes la superficie
de la tienda y del aire:
almendra azul:
uña celeste:
novia.

Turquoise, I love you
as if you were my girlfriend,
as if you were mine:
you are everywhere:
you are sparkling clean,
just recently sky blue,
just fallen from above:
you are the sky's eyes:
you slice through the surface
of the shop, of the air:
blue almond:
sky talon:
bride.

—Translated by James Nolan

After pointing out to students how Neruda addresses the color as a girlfriend, we then observe how he uses vivid verbs to tell us how turquoise moves ("just fallen from above," "you slice though the surface"). He also gives turquoise other names: blue almond, sky talon, and bride. This compact poem models for students how poets use a combination of poetic techniques to paint the exact image they want; students can also see how their previous work with "nombramientos" can be expanded just a bit further.

I also like to use Neruda's poem "X," about topaz, to illustrate the suggestive varieties of a color. It begins:

Yo te invito al topacio,
a la colmena
de la piedra amarilla,
a sus abejas,
a la miel congelada
del topacio,
a su día de oro,
a la familia
de la tranquilidad reverberante . . .

I invite you to topaz,
to the beehive
of amber stone,
to its bees,
to the congealed honey
of topaz,
to its golden day,
into the domesticity
of buzzing tranquility . . .

—*Translated by James Nolan*

After reading these poems aloud in an eighth grade bilingual class, I encouraged students to write their own color poems, particularly looking for unusual images of the color they chose. I encouraged them to be like Neruda, delving into the faraway depths of their metaphors. One student added repetition to these ideas:

Coloréame de turquesa como el hermoso Océano Pacífico.
Coloréame de turquesa como la piedra aquamarina brillante ya nacida.
Coloréame de turquesa como el más importantes de los colores traslúcidos,
Coloréame de turquesa como la sirena que se pasea en toda la costa.
Coloréame de turquesa como ojos sinceros y puros como los de niño.
Coloréame de turquesa como perla de ostión del mar precipitado.
Coloréame de turquesa como el velero que van sin rumbo.
Coloréame de turquesa porque de los más hermosos colores, ella es la más
   bella.

—*Carola Figueroa*

Color me with turquoise like the beautiful Pacific ocean.
Color me with turquoise like the shiny aquamarine stone already born.
Color me with turquoise, the most translucent of colors.

Color me with turquoise like the mermaid who passes along all the coasts.
Color me with turquoise like the sincere and pure eyes of a child.
Color me with turquoise like the oyster pearl of the deepest sea.
Color me with turquoise like a sailing ship without direction.
Color me with turquoise because it is the most beautiful of all the colors.

> —*Translated by Carol Bearse*

As in most translations, Carola's poem loses some of its beauty in English. In Spanish the sounds flow like the ocean she writes about. Observe also how she has tied together all her images relating to the sea. When she wrote, her pencil just flowed over the page, pouring out word after word, with only minor revisions later. Like Neruda, she explores a color from many angles. Her most unusual comparisons—to a mermaid and a sailing ship without direction—push her color into another dimension.

Similarly, in an eighth grade English class, after hearing Neruda's color poems, Jason Meeker, an eighth grader, wrote this haunting prose poem:

> Black is midnight. Black is the color of bats who come out at night and fly the midnight sky. Black is the color of Death. Black is a very powerful color. Black is the color of the God of Death's Kingdom. Black is my anger which builds deep inside me. Black clouds cloud my mind when I am angry. Black can be used as a weapon of Hurt.

Often for adolescents, who seem to pass the day jumping from emotion to emotion, expressing feelings is awkward and "not cool." For Jason, who was often angry and argumentative, this poem was a breakthrough for both him and his writing.

Odes: Learning from Neruda

Writing odes is a natural outgrowth of poems of address. An ode often glorifies its subject using lofty language; it is a poem of praise. To introduce odes, I read examples from Neruda's *Odas elementales* (*Odes to Simple Things*). In these poems, he writes about watermelons, shoes, socks, storms, bananas, love, family, Chile, and Guatemala, awakening us to the everyday wonders around us.

Before writing, we read "Oda al limón" ("Ode to the Lemon"). In the following excerpt, Neruda turns the ordinary into the extraordinary:

> De aquellos azahares
> desatados
> por la luz de la luna,

de aquel
olor de amor
exasperado,
hundido en la fragrancia,
salió
del limonero el amarillo,
desde su planetario
bajaron a la tierra los limones.

¡Tierna mercadería!
Se llenaron las costas,
los mercados,
de luz, de oro
silvestre,
y abrimos
dos mitades
de milagro,
ácido congelado
que corría
desde los hemisferios
de una estrella,
y el licor más profundo
de la naturaleza,
intransferible, vivo,
irreductible,
nació de la frescura
del limón,
de su casa fragrante,
de su ácida, secreta simetría.

From **Ode to the Lemon**

Out of those lemon flowers
loosed
in the moonlight,
out of that
smell of love
turned bitter,
steeped in fragrance,
yellow
burgeoned from the tree:
down from their planetarium,
lemons fell to earth.

Tender merchandise!
Piles cover harbors,
market squares,
for the light and the barbarous gold.
with light, with gold
of a miracle,
growing wild
as we open
two halves
of a miracle,
frozen acid
that streamed
from hemispheres
of a star,
and a creation's most
primal liquid,
unchangeable, living,
irreducible,
sprang from the freshness
of lemon,
from its fragrant house,
its acerbic, secret symmetry.

   —Translated by Julio Marzán

Students can experience not only the extraordinary language of this ode, but the poet's passion. Because of this passion, the poet addresses the lemon as though its very essence had transformed his soul.

I then asked students to choose an object that they felt passionate about, that transformed their lives. They began the poem by addressing the object, adding lines that glorify all its wonderful qualities. To encourage parallel structure, I suggested that they begin with their object, then write three or four lines of praise (one stanza), then repeat with another set of praise lines. As Neruda did, they can vary the number of lines but still keep within the basic structure. In the following "Ode to Night," Karla, a seventh grade bilingual student, celebrates its peace and beauty:

Noche,
viniste sola en el aire
como guitarra volante
llena de brisas

que me acariciaban en la noche.
Tus grandes ojos
me miraban desde la ventana.
Llegaste con pequeñas lágrimas
que refrescaron la naturaleza.
Llegaste oscura y desolada
como la capa del día,
siempre alumbrada
por pequeñas estrellas brillantes.
Las flores bailaban
con tu pequeña brisa
y tu hermosa luna brillante
me acompanaba en mis sueños.

   —*Karla Figueroa, seventh grade*

Night,
you came alone in the air
like a flying guitar,
full of breezes
that caressed me in the night.
Your great eyes
watched me from the window.
You came with small tears
that refreshed nature.
Night,
you came dark and desolate
like the cape of the day
always illuminated by small bright stars.
The flowers danced with your small breeze
and your beautiful, bright moon
came with me in my dreams.

   —*Translated by Carol Bearse*

In seventh grade English classes, I have presented Neruda's odes in the same manner as I did in my bilingual classes. Students are challenged to make the ordinary extraordinary by addressing objects the way Neruda does socks, shoes, and lemons. Figures 1 and 2 show how Julie Lauenger and Adam Mittleman rose to the challenge, and later incorporated art into their final draft writing of their odes. Whenever possible, I encourage students to couple art with poetry, extending their images from words into paint.

I also read to students an ode of my own, influenced by Neruda. I want my students, at a crucial time in their lives, to see that I read many poets and try on many voices to develop my own writing.

A different kind of Neruda ode, entitled "El hijo" ("The Son"), inspired students to address people or subjects. I like to introduce this ode after we have written several about seasons or objects, giving students time to develop their techniques of address and personification. I projected the poem on the overhead:

El hijo

Ay hijo, sabes, sabes
de dónde vienes?

De un lago con gaviotas
blancas y hambrientas.

Junto al agua de invierno
ella y yo levantamos
una fogata roja
gastándonos los labios
de besarnos el alma,
echando al fuego todo,
quemándonos la vida.

Así llegaste al mundo.

Pero ella para verme
y para verte un día
atravesó los mares
y yo para abrazar
su pequeña cintura
toda la tierra anduve,
con guerras y montañas,
con arenas y espinas.

Así llegaste al mundo.

The Son

Ah, son, do you know, do you know
where you came from?

From a lake with white
and hungry gulls.

Next to the water of winter
she and I raised
a red bonfire
wearing out our lips
from kissing each other's souls,
casting all into the fire
burning our lives.
That's how you came into the world.

But she, to see me,
and to see you, one day
crossed the seas
and I, to clasp
her tiny waist,
walked all the earth
with wars and mountains,
with sand and thorns.

That's how you came into the world.

Translated by Donald D. Walsh

We discussed this poem, and then I asked students to choose a person
or subject that they were truly passionate about and to write an ode prais-
ing all that person's qualities, using the highest form of comparisons.

The poetic form of the ode liberated these seventh graders to write
about their deepest feelings. They wrote odes to sadness, to their mothers
or aunts, to their boyfriends. Some chose sports or the arts to praise. I was
touched by the number of odes written to mothers; I rediscovered, through
these odes, the importance of family and relationships to all adolescents.

The following are a few of my favorites from this lesson:

Ode to My Brother

Billy,
You came with the seventh summer I
lived, life has not been the same since. I
can't even imagine life without you.
Billy,
You have an unforgettable look on your
face whenever you have mischief planned.
You take all my positions. You always try
to look innocent, but you don't fool me.
Billy,

I could not live without you. You stand
out from anyone else your age I know.
I can't help but smile whenever I see you.
Billy,
You have a million dollar smile. You have
dimples on your slightly chubby cheeks.
You are really daddy's boy.
Billy,
You look just like me when I was your age.
The spaces in your teeth make you look
even cuter than you are.
Billy,
Your hands move flowingly as you sign to
me. Your hearing aids loop around your small
ears. You're always there whenever I am sad,
even though you don't know why. You're always
there for me. Thank you.

  —Amy Sunners, seventh grade

Baseball,
you give me something to
look forward to when it's
winter,
when spring comes I've
got the fever,
when summer's here it's
the All-Star game and I love
to see all my favorite players
playing on the same team
laughing and just having fun.
When fall comes, I can
feel the World Series nearby
in my soul.
Baseball,
when I play you the rest of
the world is shut out and
nothing else matters.
When I play I'm focused to
the highest point.

I play with love, joy, and enthusiasm.
When I play, I love the feel of the game.
Baseball,
I'll play you all my life.
Baseball,
you are my pride and joy.
Baseball is my life.

—*Pat Eason, seventh grade*

An Ode to Dance

Dance,
You keep me busy every spare moment I have.
Your leaps take me into the air and let my emotions explode.
Your grace gives me challenges.
Dance,
Your many ways of expressing feelings through all types of dance thrill me.
Your challenges take my mind off all of my problems.
Your flowing movements keep me entertained
while watching you.
Dance,
Your pirouettes spin me like a top whirling and
whirling around.
Your kicks are like fireworks bursting into the air.
Your shuffles and pick-ups are music to my ears.
Dance,
I can express my feelings through you.
I don't know what I would do without you.
I need you, for you are my life.

—*Heidi Kellner, seventh grade*

Questions: Connecting Reality with Surreality

Neruda's *Book of Questions* is filled with poems that ask questions with no answers, questions that go beyond the everyday world. When I discovered this book a few years ago, I could see its potential for developing both students' imaginations and poetic technique. As students explore Neruda's questions, they often discover kernels of reality hidden within them. As they write their own pairs of questions and answers, they often discover surprises about the world around them.

I introduce this lesson by putting some of Neruda's questions on the overhead, and by giving students copies in both Spanish and English. Here is one of my favorites:

LXXII

Si todos los ríos son dulces
de dónde saca sal el mar?

Cómo saben las estaciones
que deben cambiar de camisa?

Por qué tan lentas en invierno
y tan palpitantes después?

Y luego saludar las raíces
que deben subir a la luz?

Y luego saludar al aire
con tantas flores y colores?

Siempre es la misma primavera
la que repite su papel?

   —Pablo Neruda

If all rivers are sweet,
where does the sea get its salt?

How do the seasons know
they must change their shirt?

Why so slowly in winter
and later with such a rapid shudder?

And how do the roots know
they must climb toward the light?

And then greet the air
with so many flowers and colors?

Is it always the same spring
who revives her role?

   —Translated by William O'Daly

Another one deals with the horrors of the Holocaust:

LXX

Cuál es el trabajo forzado
de Hitler en el infierno?

Pinta paredes o cadáveres?
Olfatea el gas de sus muertos?

Le dan a comer las cinizas
de tantos niños calcinados?

O le han dado desde su muerte
de beber sangre en un embudo?

O le martillan en la boca
los arrancados dientes de oro?

　　—*Pablo Neruda*

What forced labor
does Hitler do in hell?

Does he paint walls or cadavers?
Does he sniff the fumes of the dead?

Do they feed him the ashes
of so many burnt children?

Or, since his death, have they given him
blood to drink from a funnel?

Or do they hammer into his mouth
the pulled gold teeth?

—*Translated by William O'Daly*

This ode sparks lots of discussion about social injustice. Are there any answers to the horrors of war or racism? Are there any answers to the isolation and fear in which we live?

In one eighth grade class, I asked students to write their own questions, exploring both the natural world and the issues that confront them every day. Most students chose to write about the "real" world around them, thus connecting the reality of words to the sometimes unanswerable questions of inequities that permeate adolescents' subconscious wonderings.

If there were no colors, would there be peace?
If there were no violence, what would life be like?

If there were no guns, would there be murder?
If there were no drugs, would we have addicts?
If there were no Love in the world, would we still care?

   —*Noel Hernández, eighth grade*

If all people were the same, would the earth have any color?
If cats could fly, would people wonder why?
If people couldn't cry, would rain still fall from the sky?
If heartache and tears combined with your fears, would people run from their
   shadows?
If hope was a thing of the past, would love still last?

   —*Lynn Wood, eighth grade*

What if there were no playgrounds, where would all the children play?
Or would they play on the streets of a rough city and start selling drugs?

What if there were no sun, where would all the light come from?
Will it come from the moon, stars, or other planets?

What if we all had love, where would all the hate go?
Would we be nothing and go out of people's minds forever?

What if the earth stopped spinning, what would it become?
Will it become a big ball of nonexisting mass?

What if we all were one, would there be another?

   —*Edward Allen, eighth grade*

Bibliography

Cisneros, Sandra. *The House on Mango Street.* New York: Vintage Books, 1989.

Carlson, Lori, editor. *Cool Salsa: Bilingual Poems on Growing Up Latino in the United States.* New York: Henry Holt & Co., 1994.

García Lorca, Francisco and Donald Allen, editors. *The Selected Poems of García Lorca.* New York: New Directions, 1955.

García Lorca, Federico. *Canciones y poemas para niños.* San Juan, Puerto Rico: Editorial Labor, 1993.

Neruda, Pablo. *The Book of Questions.* Edited by William O'Daly. Port Townsend, Wash.: Copper Canyon Press, 1991.

————. *The Captain's Verses (Los versos del capitán).* Translated by Donald D. Walsh. New York: New Directions, 1972.

————. *Stones of the Sky.* Port Townsend, Wash.: Copper Canyon Press, 1987.

————. "The Word." In *Lives on the Line: The Testimony of Contemporary Latin American Authors.* Edited by Doris Meyer. Berkeley: University of California Press, 1988.

Soto, Gary. *A Fire in My Hands.* New York: Scholastic, 1990.

Sound, Rhythm, Music

Using a Poem by Nicolás Guillén

I like to use models when I'm trying to let my elementary school students see the terrific textures that are possible in language. Using models is important not only because it adds energy to students' writing, but also because when they write more energetic lines, they find them easier to remember and to read out loud with gusto.

One particularly useful model, involving magic and incantation, is by the Cuban poet Nicolás Guillén:

Sensemayá

Mayombé—bombe—mayombé!
Mayombé—bombe—mayombé!
Mayombé—bombe—mayombé!

La culebra tiene los ojos de vidrio;
la culebra viene y se enreda en un palo;
con sus ojos de vidrio, en un palo
con sus ojos de vidrio.
La culebra camina sin patas;
la culebra se esconde en la yerba;
caminando se esconde en la yerba;
caminando sin patas.

Mayombé—bombe—mayombé!
Mayombé—bombe—mayombé!
Mayombé—bombe—mayombé!

Tú le das con el hacha, y se muere:
dale ya!
No le des con el pie, que te muerde,
no le des con el pie, que se va!

Sensemayá, la culebra,
sensemayá.

Sensemayá, con sus ojos,
sensemayá.
Sensemayá, con su lengua,
sensemayá.
Sensemayá, con su boca,
sensemayá . . .

La culebra muerta no puede comer;
la culebra muerta no puede silbar;
no puede caminar;
no puede correr.
La culebra muerta no puede mirar;
la culebra muerta no puede beber;
no puede respirar,
no puede morder!

Mayombé—bombe—mayombé!
Sensemayá, la culebra . . .
Mayombé—bombe—mayombé!
Sensemayá, no se mueve . . .
Mayombé—bombe—mayombé!
Sensemayá la culebra . . .
Mayombé—bombe—mayombé!
Sensemayá, se murió!

—*Nicolás Guillén*

Sensemayá (Song to Kill a Snake)

Mayombé—bombe—mayombé!
Mayombé—bombe—mayombé!
Mayombé—bombe—mayombé!

The snake has eyes of glass;
the snake comes and wraps around a stick;
with its eyes of glass, on a stick,
with its eyes of glass.
The snake walks without feet;
the snake hides in the grass;
walking, it hides in the grass,
walking without feet.

Mayombé—bombe—mayombé!
Mayombé—bombe—mayombé!
Mayombé—bombe—mayombé!

You hit it with an ax and it dies:
Hit it now!
Don't hit it with your foot, or it'll bite you,
don't hit it with your foot, or it'll run!

Sensemayá, the snake, the snake,
sensemayá.
Sensemayá, with its eyes,
sensemayá.
Sensemayá, with its tongue,
sensemayá.
Sensemayá, with its mouth,
sensemayá . . .

The dead snake can't eat;
the dead snake can't hiss;
it cannot walk,
it cannot run.
The dead snake can't see;
the dead snake can't drink;
it cannot breathe,
it cannot bite!

Mayombé—bombe—mayombé!
Sensemayá, the snake, the snake . . .
Mayombé—bombe—mayombé!
Sensemayá doesn't move . . .
Mayombé—bombe—mayombé!
Sensemayá, the snake, the snake . . .
Mayombé—bombe—mayombé!
Sensemayá is dead!

—Translated by William Bryant Logan

After reading the poem aloud and talking about poems as magic, I ask the students to imagine writing a poem that would compel an animal to act in a certain way. The students and I think of examples of the repetition of words, phrases, and names that exercise a power over the hearer. Finally, I suggest that the students include a refrain of pure sound—musical, guttural, whatever—as a sort of *coup de grâce* to make the spell effective.

With this idea, I've gotten songs to Elevate an Elephant, to Sauté a Sloth, to Tame a Horse, to Put a Hippo to Sleep, to Make a Fish Swim to the Center of the Sea. Using the repetition of names and syntax and a refrain of pure sounds, the poems are always energetic. But there was one unexpected result, as well: the kids who have more trouble writing exact, concrete imagery seem to be freed by this writing idea. I don't know why, but the environment of nonsense words seems to help some of them see more clearly what they describe.

Salmon, red, salmon, orange.
Red and orange.
Salmon, red and orange.
Its name is Fish of the Sea.

Shobop beebop shobop beebop
shobop beebop shobop beebop
shoooooooooooooooobop

He flows into the center of the sea.
He flows there to catch his prey.
In the center of the sea,
to catch his prey.

The Fish of the Sea is red and orange.
Shobop beebop shooooooobop
To catch his prey in the center of the sea.

The Fish of the Sea swims fast and steadily.
The Fish of the Sea goes
to the center of the sea,
to the center of the sea,
to catch his prey.

—April Lowenthal, fifth grade

Even kids whose native language is not Spanish or English can have special fun with this technique. Maybe the pure sounds somehow connect them with their native languages. The following author is Iranian:

Eeeeeeeeeeeeeeeee
bom bom bom bom

The horse is black.
His neck is blue.
He jumps like a train.
He jumps like a rabbit.

Eeeeeeeeeeeeeeeee
bom bom bom bom

—Marwan Younis, fifth grade

Bibliography

Nicolás Guillén. *Sóngoro cosongo.* Buenos Aires: Editorial Losada, 1952.

David Mills

Ritmo y vida / Rhythm and Life
A Voyage with Lorca

The lesson plans that I enjoy are ones that teach me as much as, if not more than, my students. One that provides me with that opportunity is based on Federico García Lorca's poem "Song of Negroes in Cuba." Spanish is not my first language, but I studied it in junior high and high school and I have traveled in Guatemala, Venezuela, Spain, and Mexico (where I taught English). One thing I noticed while visiting these countries is that although Spanish is the primary language, each place has its own cultural and linguistic nuances. So when I have a bilingual poetry residency in the New York City schools, on the first day I ask the students where they are from. There might be a significant number from one country, such as the Dominican Republic, but there will also be students from Mexico, Panama, Puerto Rico, or Costa Rica. And I can't assume that because they all speak Spanish that they have the same cultural experiences or linguistic fluency.

Early in the residency, I use Lorca's surreal list poem, "Song of Negroes in Cuba," to find out about my students' native countries and to provide myself with some cultural anchors. And because I am not a native speaker, the straightforward list style of this poem allows me to present a poetry exercise and refresh my Spanish at the same time.

I tell the students that García Lorca was from Spain, and he wrote a popular book of folk poetry called *The Gypsy Ballads*, and he also wrote plays. In 1929 he came to New York to attend Columbia University. I tell them that Lorca must have felt wonder, fear, and awe while roaming the streets of New York because this was the first foreign country he had visited—and he spoke no English. I tell my students these things to help them find some common ground with Lorca and his poem.

While in New York, Lorca wrote a lot of poems that were compiled in a book he called *Poet in New York*. My idea for the class is that we too are going to be "Spanish" poets in New York. The Lorca poem we are going to examine, "Song of the Black Cubans," is about his upcoming trip to Santiago, a Cuban port. Initially, I read the poem aloud in Spanish. I tell

David Mills

the students that if they hear a repeated phrase, to say it with me.

Son de negros en Cuba

Cuando llegue la luna llena iré a Santiago de Cuba
iré a Santiago
en un coche de agua negra.
Iré a Santiago.
Cantarán los techos de palmera.
Iré a Santiago.
Cuando la palma quiere ser cigüeña,
iré a Santiago.
Y cuando quiere ser medusa el plátano,
iré a Santiago.
Iré a Santiago,
con la rubia cabeza de Fonseca.
Iré a Santiago.
Y con la rosa de Romeo y Julieta
iré a Santiago.
¡Oh Cuba! ¡Oh ritmo de semillas secas!
Iré a Santiago.
¡Oh cintura caliente y gota de madera!
Iré a Santiago.
Arpa de troncos vivos. Caimán. Flor de tabaco.
Iré a Santiago.
Siempre he dicho que yo iría a Santiago
en un coche de agua negra.
Iré a Santiago.
Brisa y alcohol en las ruedas,
iré a Santiago.
Mi coral en la tiniebla,
iré a Santiago.
El mar ahogado en la arena,
iré a Santiago,
calor blanco, fruta muerta,
iré a Santiago.
¡Oh bovino frescor de cañaveras!
¡Oh Cuba! ¡Oh curva de suspiro y barro!
Iré a Santiago.

The students do call out "iré a Santiago," and we discuss repetition as a poetic device. I tell them repetition often gives form to a poem, lending it a musicality. And that this particular refrain gives Lorca's poem a sort of call-and-response quality. Sometimes during the recitation this quality leads to a little table- or toe-tapping. In one class of sixth graders, instead of saying "Iré a Santiago" as the refrain, they all said "Amen."

I also read the poem in English:

Song of the Black Cubans

When the full moon rises
I'll go to Santiago de Cuba.
I'll go to Santiago
in a black water car.
I'll go to Santiago.
The palm leaf roofs will sing.
I'll go to Santiago.
When the palm tree wants to be a stork.
I'll go to Santiago.
And the banana tree a jellyfish.
I'll go to Santiago.
With Fonseca's blond head.
I'll go to Santiago.
And Romeo and Juliet's rose.
I'll go to Santiago.
Paper sea and coin silver.
I'll go to Santiago.
Oh Cuba, oh rhythm of dry seeds!
I'll go to Santiago.
Oh hot waist and drop of wood!
I'll go to Santiago.
Harp of living tree trunks,
cayman, tobacco flower!
I'll go to Santiago.
I always said I'd go to Santiago
in a black water car.
I'll go to Santiago.
Alcohol and breeze in the wheels.
I'll go to Santiago.
My coral in the darkness.
I'll go to Santiago.
The sea drowned in the sand.
I'll go to Santiago.
White heat, dead fruit.
I'll go to Santiago.
Oh bovine freshness of reeds!

153

Oh Cuba! Oh curve of sighs and clay!
I'll go to Santiago.

—Translated by William Bryant Logan

We talk about what translation means and why the same poem sounds so different, how Spanish as a language seems to have more music and rhythm than English.

I discuss the lines that surround the repeated line "iré a Santiago." One student invariably asks, "How does he go to Cuba in a black water car, what is a black water car?"

And I tell them that a car of black water can be anything they want it to be. I explain that this type of image is what is called surrealist. And I explain that surrealism is when things go beyond the real and into another world. "The books danced on the ceiling when the students left the room," is an example of surrealism. I ask them to find other examples of surrealism in Lorca's poem. "Palm thatch will sing," a student says.

"Yes! And who or what else can sing?"

"People!"

This provides me with a good opportunity to introduce the idea of personification.

Then I bring in some more background for the poem. I tell them that Lorca found New York to be a tough place—he actually lived here during the early part of the Great Depression. I explain that that was when the stock market crashed and there was a lot of poverty and few jobs. I ask them what they now see in New York that might be similiar to the great depression. We discuss homelessness. "What does Lorca notice about Cuba?" I ask.

"The land!"

"'The sea drowned in sand.'"

"'Curve of sighs and clay.'"

"What else does he notice?" I ask.

"The fruits!"

"The music!"

"'The rhythm of dry seeds.'"

"Like maracas!"

"Although Lorca liked Cuba more than New York, is there any description of Santiago that is not positive?"

"Yeah when he talks about the white heat and fruit rot."

"O.K., now I want you to help me make a short list of things in New

York that are different from things in the country you came from."

In New York:
weather
traffic
concrete
people not as polite
everything fast

Then I ask the students to close their eyes and imagine that it is the dead of winter, snow everywhere, and they are heading to JFK airport. They arrive at their terminal and board the plane. They take a flight to their country. I ask them to imagine that they are now back "home" and to open their eyes there: "What is one of the first things you see? Take out a sheet of paper and write it down. What type of music might you hear? What flowers might you smell? What would the weather be like? What foods might you eat? What is the name of the town you used to live in? What family member greets you?"

I then ask them to write a poem using the repetitive line "I'll go to" and use the name of their hometown. I ask them to try to make some of the things in their hometown do surreal things. I tell them I want to feel like I have just been to their hometowns after reading their poems:

Going to Puebla

I'll leave New York's cold concrete
And go to Puebla in a 747
I'll go to Puebla
And the sun will smile on my house
I'll go to Puebla
And Popocatepetl will scratch the clouds
I'll go to Puebla
And my uncle Juan Carlos will drive me on the curvy roads
I'll go to Puebla
And I'll make a sombrero from tortillas
I'll go to Puebla
And hear the mariachis play polka music for fiesta
I'll go to Puebla
And drink pulque with my uncle
I'll go to Puebla
I'll go to Puebla
I'll be home

     —Carlos G., sixth grade

As with Lorca's poem, I have each author read the detailed lines and the class recite the refrain.

Bibliography

For another translation of Lorca's poem, see *Poet in New York,* translated by Greg Simon and Steven F. White, edited by Christopher Maurer. New York: The Noonday Press, 1995.

David Unger

Antonio Machado's "Childhood Memory"

Antonio Machado's "Recuerdo infantil" ("Childhood Memory") is a wonderful poem for classroom use either in its Spanish original or in English translation. Due to the poem's subject matter—a school experience—and its layers of meaning, I've had much success using this poem with students from fifth to twelfth grade.

Before discussing the poem, I tell the students a little something about Machado: that he was born in Seville, Spain, in 1875, that he was himself a French teacher and became the leading writer of the "Generation of '98" poets. His poetry was an attempt to use simple language to reveal his own interior landscape. Then I call on students to read the poem in both languages, first in English (since most of my students' first language is English) to get a sense of the meaning, and then in Spanish (if there is a decent Spanish reader in the class), to hear how Machado phrased that meaning. Here's the poem:

Childhood Memory

A cold and overcast winter
afternoon. The students
are studying. Endless boredom
of rain beyond the windowpanes.

It is time for class. In a poster
Cain is seen running
off, and Abel dead,
lying beside a red spot.

With a deep and hollow voice,
the teacher is thundering, an old man
badly dressed, withered and dry,
with a book in his hand.

And the whole children's choir
is singing its lesson:
"Thousand times one hundred, a hundred thousand,
thousand times one thousand, a million."

A cold and overcast winter
afternoon. The students
are studying. Endless boredom
of rain on the windowpanes.

—Translated by David Unger

Recuerdo infantil

Una tarde parda y fría
de invierno. Los colegiales
estudian. Monotonía
de lluvia tras los cristales.

Es la clase. En un cartel
se representa a Caín
fugitivo, y muerto Abel
junto a una mancha carmín.

Con timbre sonoro y hueco
truena el maestro, un anciano
mal vestido, enjuto y seco,
que lleva un libro en la mano.

Y todo un coro infantil
va cantando la lección:
Mil veces ciento, cien mil,
mil veces mil, un millón.

Una tarde parda y fría
de invierno. Los colegiales
estudian. Monotonía
de la lluvia en los cristales.

"Recuerdo infantil" recounts a childhood memory, in this case, Machado's own. The poem is set in a school classroom and the images of the opening stanza set the darkened, almost stifling atmosphere of the poem: it is an overcast and cold winter afternoon, with rain falling. Stanza two describes one aspect of the interior space of the classroom: it's a poster of Cain fleeing his brother Abel, who is lying, apparently dead, next to a red spot or puddle (you might have to explain who Cain and Abel are). What kind of mood does this poster create? In a strange way, the poster is there to frighten the schoolchildren, to warn them where unleashed jealousy or passion might lead. You could ask your kids how they would feel about having a poster such as this in their classroom. What kind of posters do they have in their classroom(s)? Do their "brightness" and "warmth" help them feel good about themselves and life in general?

Notice how Machado is painting a fuller picture line by line. Stanza three introduces us to the teacher who is conducting his lesson, not in a soft or gentle voice, but in a voice like thunder. What kind of response does a "thundering" voice elicit? The teacher is an old man, "badly dressed" and "dried up." What do the images "thundering" and "dried up" tell us about the narrator's feelings toward the teacher? What does the book in his hand represent? Would he be capable of conducting the lesson without a book? What would happen to him if he tried?

Stanza four introduces the "difficult" math lesson that demands that the teacher hold the book! They are repeating a "times" table. Did the students notice that Machado refers to the schoolchildren as a children's choir? What ideas is he trying to convey? Can we conjecture what Machado might think about "rote" or "by-the-book" learning?

The last stanza, as in many rock, rap, or folk songs, repeats the first one. But are the stanzas identical? Notice how Machado gives resonance to the last stanza by slightly altering the image of the rain: it is no longer falling outside the window but instead dripping down the glass, the way tears streak a face. It is a somber ending, with no sense of escape. Not the kind of classroom we teachers like to envision.

You can ask older students to talk more specifically about the poem's structure or construction. "Recuerdo infantil" has five quatrains. The *abab cdcd* etc. rhyme scheme is fluid and Machado's use of enjambment keeps the poem from having a sing-song quality. Internal rhymes help to echo certain words that mirror the death-like order in the classroom. The syllabic count, mostly between eight and ten syllables, tends to run in patterns, which is emphasized by the climactic penultimate stanza's being the only one with seven-count lines. The last stanza is exactly like the first one, except that Machado has added two counts to the final line, which reinforces the poem's closure and the sense of hopeless repetition.

Writing Lesson

While we would like childhood to be happy, we know that children are all cursed with some bad or embarrassing memories as well. The Machado poem allows students to feel that they can write about unpleasant experiences, to exteriorize events or incidents that caused them pain. Depending on their ages and sophistication, I ask students to write a poem that recounts a painful or amusing experience in school or some other childhood memory. Though I encourage them to choose something that happened to them, I will also accept something that happened to someone they know or an account of an incident they observed.

Here are a few poems that my students wrote in response to the Machado poem.

School

The sun's rays entering
through the window.
A cool breeze floating
in the air.

Silence surrounding us
while we bend down
over our work.

A teacher looking
around and walking
back and forth.

Doors slamming in
the hallway.
Cars passing by
outside.

The bell suddenly
rings
and the period ends.

Noise bursts in
and our silence ends
like an enemy army
that has invaded our silence.

—*Yanitza Tavárez, middle school*

School Boredom

Sitting in the chair with nothing
to do. Just listen to Mr. Do
and looking out the window seeing
the snow coming down.

It is time for reading and
getting more bored. The same as
always. Just sitting like stones
without a move. You have to
stay calm.

The teacher is talking and
saying what an excellent book
we are reading. The students
just saying well, yes, Mr. Do,
what an excellent book, but
really we know it is
a boring and uninteresting book.

Sitting in the chair with nothing
to do. Just listen to Mr. Do
and looking out the window seeing
the snow coming down.

—*Ivelise Rodríguez, middle school*

El primer día de escuela

I was frightened
like a little fly
among a swarm of bees.

I was lonely
as a rose among a dozen daisies.
The teachers were
very simpático with me.
I worked very hard and felt
like a balloon without air.

The teacher asked me a question,
I didn't know the answer
and felt like a boat
without its sails.

161

The day ended and I was as happy
as a flower blooming
on the first day of spring.

The first day of school
I was frightened
like a little fly
among a swarm

                     of

                              bees.

    —*Wendy Pérez, middle school*

Bibliography

Machado, Antonio. *Poesías.* Buenos Aires: Losada, 1943.

JANINE POMMY VEGA

A Moment of Change
Using a Poem by Juan Ramón Jiménez

In the first several sessions with students, I cover some basic ground: metaphor and simile; the use of the five senses in description; and the idea of the persona poem wherein the interior of a character is as important as the world he, she, or it inhabits. This last I usually illustrate by picturing the largeness of the universe around oneself as equal to that of the universe within. The private world inside us contains our feelings, thoughts, secrets, memories, and dreams. I put both these worlds on the board: the five senses connecting us with the outer world, and at least five aspects of the internal world.

By this time the kids have gotten on a roll, in terms of creativity, and have come to trust me. Then I can bring in the following poem.

Mares

Siento que el barco mío
ha tropezado, allá en el fondo,
con algo grande!
                                    Y nada
sucede! Nada . . . Quietud . . . Olas...

—Nada sucede; o es que ha sucedido todo,
 y estamos ya, tranquilos, en lo nuevo?

   —*Juan Ramón Jiménez*

Oceans

I have a feeling that my boat
has struck, down there in the depths,
against a great thing.
                                    And nothing
happens! Nothing . . . Silence . . . Waves . . .

—Nothing happens? Or has everything happened,
and are we standing now, quietly, in the new life?

   —*Translated by Robert Bly*

163

In class I change the last word to "way," which is also correct and better suits the lesson.

This poem works well with writers from fourth grade up. In a bilingual class, or a high school Spanish class, I make sure all the examples I bring are in both English and Spanish, and that there are enough photocopies for everyone. I read the poem in Spanish as well as English, so the students can hear its original music.

After I read the poem aloud, I ask if anybody understands it. I usually get a no. I explain that when something happens to us—something from the outside, or from the inside, like the first time one perceives cruelty in the world, or realizes one's own beauty—there is an absolute change in one's entire being. You may look the same, and act the same, but inside, you are different. You are changed.

If I am your friend, I can perhaps read something in your face, but otherwise unless you choose to tell me about it, the change remains entirely in your own private world. On the outside, apparently nothing has happened. I illustrate this with the example of the first time you realize Santa Claus does not exist, that somebody else leaves the toys.

Then I bring up another amazing fact. The way we human beings are built, we remember best when strong emotions are involved. If you're having a boring day today, in two years you will not remember it. But if your father has chosen today to leave your home and never come back, this day will be a memory that sticks to you; it becomes part of who you are.

I ask them to think back to a moment when something happened outside themselves, or something changed inside. We share the kids' poems I've brought in to illustrate. At this point I usually ask for volunteers to read them in both languages.

The following examples by students were written in English and translated by me into Spanish:

When My Father Left

When my father left, I was four,
and my brother was one.
As he went out, everything
began to get quiet. My
mother said he was only going
back to his country to stay
for a while, but we
couldn't understand her.

After he really went out, and my
mother closed the door, the house
had no sound. It wasn't cheerful
like it was when my father was
in the house. The next day
it was so quiet, it seemed
as if everyone was sleeping.

—*Verónica López, fourth grade*

Cuando se fue mi padre

Cuando se fue mi padre, yo tenía cuatro años
y mi hermanito tenía un año.
Cuando él salío, todo
comenzó a callarse. Mi madre dijo
que solamente iba a ir a su país
para quedar un rato
pero no pudimos entenderla.
Despues de que salió de veras
y mi madre cerró la puerta, la casa
no tenía sonido. No estaba alegre
como cuando mi padre estaba en casa.
El día siguiente, la casa estaba tan silenciosa,
parecía que todos dormían.

The Big Oak Tree

One time, in Santo Domingo,
my parents wanted to come
to New York
so that I could learn English.
I didn't want to come.
After dinner, I went
to a big oak tree, and let
the ants crawl over my feet.
They tickled me.
Suddenly, for some unknown
reason,
I wanted to come to New York.
If it would make my parents happy,
it would make me happy.

—*Edward Espinal, sixth grade*

El roble grande

Una vez, en Santo Domingo,
mis padres querían venir
a Nueva York
para que yo pudiera aprender Inglés.
Yo no quería venir.
Después del almuerzo, me fui
a un roble grande, y dejé
que las hormigas se arrastraran
sobre mis pies.
Me hicieron cosquillas.
De repente, por alguna razón
desconocida,
yo quería venir a Nueva York.
Si les hacía felices a mis padres,
me hacía feliz a mí.

Hard Work in Guyana

My grandfather was chopping down
sugar cane in the field,
his face and his back
were covered with sweat.
He hardly had any clothes on—
only pants, rolled up
like bluejeans.
It was my last day
before leaving my country.
When my grandfather came toward the house,
I ran to kiss him.

—*Esther Sukhdeo, eighth grade*

Trabajo duro in Guyana

Mi abuelo estaba cortando
caña de azucar en la finca
su rostro y sus espaldas
estaban cubiertos de sudor.
No llevaba mucha ropa—
solamente pantalones arrollados
como blue jeans.
Era mi último día

antes de partir de mi país.
cuando vino mi abuelo hacia la casa,
yo corrí a besarlo.

(The following translations from Spanish are also by me.)

La música
(*poem written for Spanish class*)

Sentado en frente de mi piano,
Mis dedos tocan el teclado frío
La música que hago está muy larga,
alta, rápida y completa.
Oigo el sonido de mis uñas
contra las teclas. Veo la música
volar delante de mis ojos.
Mis manos
se sienten separados de mi cuerpo.

    —*Jonathon Russo, eleventh grade*

The Music

Sitting at my piano,
My fingers touch the cold keyboard
The music I make is very long,
high, fast and complete.
I hear the sound of my nails
against the keys. I see the music
flying before my eyes.
My hands
feel separate from my body.

Recuerdo de un arbol

Fue una tarde
antes de que yo viniera
para este país,
había una mata de mango
llena de mangos maduros
en la cual yo me subía
y comía mucho. Comía tantos
mangos que no podía comer
otro más.
Y ahora cada vez

que viene la temporada de los mangos
yo me siento triste y solo
sin encontrar nada que hacer.

    —Félix de la Cruz, ninth grade

Memory of a Tree

It was one afternoon
before I came to this country,
there was a mango tree
full of ripe mangos
into which I climbed
and ate a lot. I ate so many mangos
I couldn't eat even one more.
And now every time mango season comes
I feel sad and alone
with nothing to do.

I point out that in most cases the poets do not tell us how they feel. They describe the event and let us feel something for ourselves. I ask what senses the poets have used in their poems, to make the outside or inside moment come alive. Then I tell them a story from my own life, where apparently nothing special happened, but where the memory still sticks to me. I try to incorporate at least three senses in the story. Then I ask the kids what the feeling was, and to identify what senses I used.

Now we are ready to write about a memory that has stuck with us, a moment of change that is part of the person we have become. With other assignments, I encourage students to read their own poems aloud to the class; but since this can be a highly personal poem, I suggest that I read them at the end, omitting all names unless the writer indicates otherwise. Occasionally the poems deal with very serious and sensitive issues. If the authors prefer not to have their poems read at all, I ask them to write that at the top of their poems.

Bibliography

Jiménez, Juan Ramón. In *Lorca and Jiménez: Selected Poems.* Translated by Robert Bly. Boston: Beacon Press, 1973.

Bill Zavatsky

Introducing the *Greguería*— and Ramón Gómez de la Serna

On this side of the Atlantic we are familiar with some of modern Spain's great writers—the poet Federico García Lorca, with his contemporaries Miguel Hernández and Vicente Aleixandre, winner of the Nobel Prize for Literature. But who, except for specialists, has even heard of one of the most prolific and honored writers that Spain has produced, Ramón Gómez de la Serna (1888–1963), so popular that during his heyday he was affectionately known to the reading public simply as "Ramón"? Lorca once sat at his feet, Neruda honored him with a touching ode, and almost every modernist writer in Spain and the Americas felt his influence at one time or another.

In a career that began when he was seventeen, Ramón published at least a hundred books, everything from novels to short stories to biographies of writers and artists. Of this prodigious output, Gómez de la Serna is best known for his invention of the *greguería,* a kind of aphoristic prose poem. The complete edition of these little masterpieces, called *Total de greguerías* (*All the Greguerías*), runs to nearly 1600 pages.

The word *greguería* itself, Rita (Mazzetti) Gardiol informs us, "derives from *gringo* 'in the sense of an incomprehensible language,' and was first listed officially in the *Diccionario de autoridades* in 1734, where it was defined as meaning *algarabía,* in reference to the incomprehensible Arabic language" (Gardiol 1974, 130). Ramón himself described the discovery of the *greguería* in this way:

> Then I put my hand into the great hat of words, and by chance, which ought to be the baptizer of the best finds, I turned up a ball. . . .
>
> It was "*Greguería,*" still in the singular, but I planted this tiny ball and grew a garden of *greguerías.* I took the word for its euphony and for the secrets that its sex concealed.
>
> *Greguería,* Arabic, confused outcry. (In the older dictionaries it means the squealing of piglets when they see their mama from behind.)

>What beings scream in confusion from their unconscious is what things scream. (*Total* 1962, 22–23)

What Ramón located at the heart of the *greguería* (and seemed to employ as its organizing principle) was the metaphor. Remember that in 1911, when Ramón "discovered" the *greguería,* the ripple effects of the experiment called Imagism, carried out by poets in London from 1907 to 1909, were beginning to influence the poetic practice of a number of soon-to-be-important British and American poets. Imagism cut away excessively flowery poetic language and restored the metaphor as the heart of poetry. Similar movements were afoot all over Europe during the decade or so before World War One.

In his *greguerías* Ramón is always thinking of one thing (most often, an object) in terms of another, drawing lines of connection between them, creating the "third thing"—the metaphor. He summed up this combination (in a more abstract fashion) in his formula "Humor + metaphor = *greguería*" (*Total* 35). Humor is inherent in the *greguerías,* the *delight* (even to laughter) that some of his constructions provoke. Surely there is something magical about metaphor in and of itself; it is the magician's hat out of which the unexpected rabbit is yanked. It is a piece of invention—fire bursting from two sticks that are rubbed together—and comedy all at once. We may be amazed or stunned by what Ramón has produced with a few words, but a smile, at least, lurks at the edges of his prestidigitation. "How did he *do* that?" the reader of the *greguerías* keeps asking.

The kind of seeing that Ramón does might be compared to a "poetic" pair of eyeglasses: from one lens the poet looks outward, seeing what is right in front of him in great detail, with enormous power of concentration; but in the other lens (the one that feeds into the right side of the brain, which animates the imagination) he looks inward to see something else, the "something else" to which he connects the "ordinary" object (or some unique aspect of that object). The combination, or "double vision" of the "outer" and "inner" lenses, is "resolved"—to use the oculist's term—in the "vision" of the *greguería*. The same formula, I think, could serve as an imaginative definition of the metaphor, which is not *real* in the sense that it can be scientifically verified. It is "proven" by the imagination, by the "Ah!" response provoked when the magician pulls the coin from your ear.

One last bit of theory. Since the *greguería,* a miniature form, seems to demand a nutshell definition, how about this one?: the *greguería* is an attempt at definition by metaphor. Almost every one of Ramón's *greguerías* attempts to define something: "Cheese: milk's immortality." (When a liquid goes to heaven, Ramón jokes, it achieves the densest reality on the physical scale; it becomes a solid.) Aristotle claims that "we all naturally find it agreeable to get hold of new ideas easily," adding that "it is from metaphor that we can best get hold of something fresh" (*Rhetoric* 1954, 186). It is this freshness (and the delight that it provokes) that adds the twist to Gómez de la Serna's poetic definitions called *greguerías*. And it isn't much of a leap to relate freshness and delight to humor—or to magic. Metaphor, then, supplies explanations that elude (or enhance) the dictionary, catching the truth called poetry.

But now we ought to have a few *greguerías* put in front of us, for the best way to get a feel for Gómez de la Serna's inventions is to read some examples. Below is a selection (my translations). There is a larger selection at the end of the essay.

El pez más difícil de pescar es el jabón dentro del agua.

The hardest fish to catch is soap in water.

≈

El rayo es una especie de sacacorchos encolerizado.

Lightning is a kind of furious corkscrew.

≈

Entre las satisfacciones de las médicos debe estar la de lavarse las manos con una toalla recién estrenada.

Among the satisfactions of doctors ought to be that of drying their hands with a brand-new towel.

≈

No es la esfera de los relojes. Es la córnea de las relojes.

That's not the face of the watch. It's the watch's cornea.

≈

Los colchones de borra están hechos de la pelusa que lleva la vida en los bolsillos.

Cotton mattresses are stuffed with the lint that life puts in our pockets.

≈

El rayo muestra la sutura craneana del cielo.

Lightning reveals the cranial suture of the sky.

~

Dormía con la boca abierta, como si fuese un paleto de los sueños.

He sleeps with his mouth open, as if he were a country bumpkin in his dreams.

~

Hay unas viejas que llevan el pecho lleno de alfileres negros, como en recordación de sus dolores.

There are old women who wear a chest full of black pins, like remembrances of their sorrows.

~

¡Qué tragedia! Envejecían sus manos y no envejecian sus sortijas.

What a tragedy! Her hands grew old and her rings didn't.

~

El león tiene altavoz propio.

The lion carries his own loudspeaker.

~

Un pie levanta la colcha del mar: es un delfín.

A foot lifts the bedspread of the sea: it's a dolphin.

If the act of seeing is crucial to the writing of the *greguería*, what else can we do to help our students open their eyes? Looking "outward" isn't always as simple as it might seem. Too often we don't stop to take a close look at the things around us. Many methods of instruction that can sharpen our vision are already in place in some schools: art classes, courses in art history, photography workshops. One excellent exercise for teachers and students is to take a trip to a spot in their neighborhoods to do what I call observation writing. My students and I are lucky that there is a little flower garden tended by neighborhood residents near our school. Early in September, before the weather changes, and in the spring when it warms up again, I lead my classes to the garden for a couple of writing sessions. (Any place where observation can be done—a coffee house, for example—will suffice. If students can't leave the school, take them out to the playground.) The assignment works only if students write individually and quietly: no talking, no clustering in groups, no roving around—or at least a minimum of movement, and only in order to get settled into a "good" spot from which to look.

On our first outing I urge the students to stay away from making comparisons; I want them simply to see and to report what they have observed, not to "poeticize" it by introducing similes and metaphors. Excellent poetry can be written after a close observation of what lies under our noses, whether or not one has a talent for metaphor. (Many students don't, and that's no reason why they should be made to feel that they can't write poetry.) I also "put the squelch" on metaphor-making because all too often young people have at the ready a stock of clichés that they are all too eager to apply to untrammeled observation. I don't want them telling me that the clouds look like cotton candy, or that the little bee is smiling. Before I ease my restriction, we need to discuss what metaphor is, what it does, and what clichés are. So, before we scatter into the garden, I tell them that as soon as they are tempted to see the bee in terms of something else—a little helicopter, let's say (which might be a perfectly appropriate comparison)— they should bite their tongues and either keep watching the bee, writing down what it *actually* does, or turn their attention to something else, shaking the comparison out of their heads. Most students find that they can accomplish this writing assignment successfully because (they think!) they "aren't really writing poetry."

By the time of our next field trip, usually a few days later, we will have read up on metaphor (using my essay on it in *The Teachers & Writers Handbook of Poetic Forms*) and perhaps played some of the Surrealist games that provoke the exciting conjunction of opposites. One such game is called "Surrealist Definitions." One player writes the word to be defined ("Love") or may present the thing to be defined as a title ("Love in the Moonlight"). The first player may also couch the word or phrase as a question: "What is love?" "What is love in the moonlight?" The second player, without seeing the word or title, writes a definition (a declarative sentence or a sentence fragment will do): "A battered copy of *The Concise Oxford Dictionary*." Then the two players match up the word or phrase and its new "definition."

While all of these activities prepare us for the *greguerías*, Ramón himself is the best guide. Give your students some of his *greguerías* to read and discuss. Teachers of Spanish could encourage their students to do their own translations, improving on the ones that I've offered here. There are hundreds of them to choose from. A few students will immediately pick up on the spirit of Gómez de la Serna's inventions, but allow everyone a few days to walk around and look at things with their new "eyeglasses" on as they dip in and out of Ramon's miniature masterpieces. Then have the students create some *greguerías* of their own, as did my twelfth grade students at the Trinity School in New York:

Clock: plastic sun.

Your car has disowned you when it's locked and the keys are inside.

Rain is beautiful when you are standing next to it.

If fish can cough underwater, what happens when they sneeze?

The subway train: giant earthworm.

I wonder if I'll have to wear glasses in my afterlife.

Are there fire extinguishers in hell?

   —Tony Yung

"Crazy" means bolder than I.

The W is a dash that crashed head-on into a wall.

The f is the t checking to see if its shoes are tied.

Music is the river between our ears that carries us from one emotion to another.

Although each tear holds the pain we feel, no number of tears can take that pain away.

   —Bradley Pitts

Boots are shoes with more character.

When a snowflake touches the ground, it becomes just like every other drop of water in the world.

—*Jared Gordon*

At church everybody lost their contact lenses at the same time.

Two people wandering in the dark will eventually touch each other.

—*Jon Robbins*

The wrinkles on your mother's face are the number of times you made her cry alone.

—*Claudia Freeman*

A flying saucer is never without a flying teacup.

Plagiarism is a patient etherized upon a table.

Who owns the sun? It seems like an excellent money-making venture.

Paint is the skin of a house.

The pen is the mouth of the hand.

The light bulb above my head that is an idea burned out because it was turned on too quickl—wait, what was I saying?

Inside our heads there are tiny creatures that type out our thoughts on tiny typewriters. Sometimes they make mistakes.

Who hangs up God's clothes when he comes home from work?

A cliché is red as an apple.

Cardboard is wood that doesn't want it enough.

—*John Bachman*

The most imaginative thoughts come to me as I lie in bed, too tired to write them down, lost the next morning.

Imagine shaking a book: all the images, places, people falling to the floor.

—*Taro Hashimura*

The letter Z always seems in such a rush. Perhaps it only wants to catch up with the other letters.

Sighs are buckets we use to bail grief from our sinking bodies.

—*Jamie O'Grady*

If you die in the woods and no one is there to see you die, do you really die?

Shadows are footprints of the sun.

Dead turtles move even slower.

If one of your relatives lives in a cave and mauls people when they visit, that relative is a bear!

—*Jordon Ferber*

The O is the only figure with dual citizenship.

No man will ever see a virgin forest.

—*Ben Stingle*

More Greguerías by Ramón Gómez de la Serna

Cuando además de todo hay música en un alma, bien; ¡pero cuidado con las almas sólo llenas de música!

If, in addition to everything else, a soul has music, good. But beware of souls that are full of nothing but music!

~

Las proclamas que arrojanlos aviones quieren ser en el cielo bandadas de pájaros, pero después caen como desengañadas proclamas.

Leaflets thrown from airplanes want to be flocks of birds in the sky, but instead fall down like disillusioned leaflets.

~

Al pasar junto a la cárcel sentimos que nuestra sombra—una de nuestras sombras—está en una de las celdas de un patio interior.

When we go by a jail we feel as if our shadow—one of our shadows—is in one of the cells of an inner courtyard.

~

Cuando nos sentamos a meditar al borde de la cama es cuando somos como presidiarios que reflexionan su condena.

When we sit in thought on the edge of our beds, we're like convicts thinking about their sentences.

~

En las aguas minerales burbujean peces invisibles, almas del silencio acuático, respiracíon de ranas, peces desaparecidos y últimos suspiros.

In mineral water invisible fish bubble up, the souls of aquatic silence, the breathing of frogs, extinct fish, and last gasps.

~

Para poner nuestro corazón en hora dirigimos una mirada al cielo.

To set our hearts to the correct time, we look up at the sky.

~

Los grandes reflectores buscan a Dios.

Big mirrors search for God.

~

La mano vieja se agarra a la vida como la del pájaro a la rama.

A hand that's old clings to life like a bird to the branch.

~

Los paréntesis salen de las cejas del escritor.

Parentheses emerge from the writer's eyebrows.

~

El agua no tiene memoria: por eso es tan limpia.

Water has no memory: that's why it's so clear.

~

Un epitafio es una tarjeta de desafío a la muerte.

An epitaph is a calling card handed to death.

~

El reloj es el guardapelo del tiempo.

The watch is the locket of time.

~

El mar es la rotativa más antigua del mundo, que tira incesantemente y en rotograbado el diario «La Ola».

The sea is the oldest printing press in the world, printing non-stop and with pictures the daily called *The Wave*.

~

El niño intenta extraerse las ideas por la nariz.

The little boy tries to extract his ideas through his nose.

~

La L parace largar un puntapié a la letra que lleva al lado.

The big L seems to give a kick to the letter that follows it.

~

En la noche de los vagones solitarios vamos con dos mujeres: la nuestra y la que se refleja en el cristal.

At night on a lonely train we travel with two women: the one with us and the one reflected in the glass.

~

La i es dedo meñique del alfabeto.

The i is the pinky of the alphabet.

~

La música de los discos está llena de ratones.

The music on records is full of mice.

~

La niña con el aro en la mano va al jardín como al colegio, a jugar con la circunferencia y la tangente.

The girl with a hoop in her hand goes off to the flower garden as if to school, to play with circumferences and tangents.

~

Las gaviotas nacieron de los pañuelos que dicen adiós en los puertos.

Seagulls are born from the handkerchiefs that wave goodbye at ports.

~

A las olas no les importa la lluvia, como si tuviesen impermeable.

Rain doesn't matter to the waves, as if they were waterproof.

~

El pañuelo de seda es el adiós de una caricia.

The silk scarf is the goodbye of a caress.

~

Las vacas escriben con el tintero de sus ojos el poema de la resignación.

Cows write the poem of resignation with the inkwell of their eyes.

~

Lo terrible de la muerte de los peces es que no se les puede cerrar los ojos. ¡No tienen párpados!

What is terrible about the death of fish is that they can't close their eyes. They don't have eyelids!

~

El pavo real es un mito jubilado.

The peacock is a retired myth.

~

Cuando oímos los trinos de un pájaro hacemos gárgaras por los oídos.

When we listen to the warblings of a bird, we gargle our ears.

~

Gato, la máquina fotográfica del misterio.

Cat: mystery's hidden camera.

~

El cuervo se peina antes de entrar en la ciudad.

The raven combs its hair before going into town.

~

La q es la p que vuelve de paseo.

The q is the p coming back from a walk.

~

La golondrina llega tan lejos porque es la flecha y el arco a la vez.

The swallow lands so far away because it is the both the arrow and the bow.

~

De lo que se habla en la oscuridad queda copia en papel carbono.

He who talks to himself in the dark ends up with a carbon copy of his thoughts.

~

En las estrellas no hay ni un ruiseñor.

Up among the stars there isn't a single nightingale.

~

El electricista se siente cuñado de la electricidad.

The electrician thinks that he's electricity's brother-in-law.

~

Tenía ojos de botón cosido.

He has the eyes of a tightly-sewn button.

~

Eolo es el dios de viento y el diptongo.

Aeolus is the god of the wind and of the dipthong.

~

Ascensor: prisón momentánea.

Elevator: one-minute prison.

~

El ancla se sonrie en el fondo del mar.

The anchor smiles at the bottom of the sea.

Works Cited or Mentioned

Aristotle. *Rhetoric* and *Poetics*. *Rhetoric* translated by W. Rhys Roberts. *Poetics* translated by Ingram Bywater. Introduction by Friedrich Solmsen. New York: The Modern Library, 1954.

Brotchie, Alastair, compiler. *A Book of Surrealist Games*. Edited by Mel Gooding. Translations by Alexis Lykiard and Jennifer Batchelor. Boston & London: Shambhala Redstone Editions, 1995.

Gómez de la Serna, Ramón. *Total de greguerías*. Madrid: Aguilar, 1962.

———. *Greguerías (Selección)*. Selection and introduction by Gaspar Gómez de la Serna. Salamanca: Ediciones Anaya, 1969. A paperback selection of *greguerías*.

Gardiol, Rita (Mazzetti). *Ramón Gómez de la Serna*. New York: Twayne Publishers, Inc. /Twayne World Authors Series No. 338, 1974.

Zavatsky, Bill. "Metaphor," in *The Teachers & Writers Handbook of Poetic Forms*. Edited by Ron Padgett. New York: Teachers and Writers Collaborative, 1987.

Works by Ramón Gómez de la Serna in English Translation

Gómez de la Serna, Ramón. *Dalí*. New York: William Morrow and Company, Inc., 1979. Translated from the Spanish by Nicholas Fry; other essays translated from the Italian by Elisabeth Evans. Ramón's unfinished essay (25 pages) as well as essays by others on Gómez de la Serna and Dalí, a Dalí chronology, illustrations of 68 works by Dalí, and other materials.

————. *Some Greguerías.* Translated by Helen Granville-Barker. New York: n.p., but "Printed by William E. Rudge's Sons" appears on final page, 1944.

————. *Greguerías: The Wit and Wisdom of Ramón Gómez de la Serna.* Selected, introduced, and translated by Philip Ward. Cambridge, England, and New York: The Oleander Press, 1982. One of two available anthologies of *greguerías* currently available in book form.

————. *Movieland.* Translated from the Spanish by Angel Flores. New York: The Macaulay Company, 1930.

————. *The Gentleman with "It."* New York: The American Guild, n.d. One wonders if indeed this book, cited in bibliographies, was ever published at all.

————. *Aphorisms.* Selected, translated and introduced by Miguel Gonzalez-Gerth. Pittsburgh, Pennsylvania: Latin American Literary Review Press / Series: Discoveries, 1989. This is the other, and quite good, translation of selected *greguerías* currently in print.

Other translations into English in anthologies and periodicals appearing between 1923 and 1933 are cited by Rodolfo Cardona in his valuable book called *Ramón: A Study of Gómez de la Serna and His Works* (New York: Eliseo Torres & Sons, 1957).

NAOMI SHIHAB NYE

Día de dulce / Sweet Day
Using Paz, Pacheco, Gutiérrez, Deltoro, & Blanco

In San Antonio's inner city, the streets are shaded by huge aging pecan trees. It's hard to take a walk without nuts crunching underfoot. (*Students, do you notice them? Are you so used to their sounds you don't notice anymore?*)

The giant Judson Candy Factory on South Flores Street has been silent for nineteen years. Too bad. The whole air used to smell like rich chocolate around here. (*Does your grandma or mom remember it? What do you think they were dreaming of when they used to smell that smell?*)

But the Segovia Mexican Candy factory down on Guadalupe Street has been churning out mounds of pralines since 1918 and the salsa has grown tastier in Mexican cafés since more people seem to have developed a taste for the *chipotle* pepper, and the Sanitary Tortilla Factory a few blocks away is bustling. Hot brown paper sacks filled with stacks of freshly pressed corn tortillas replenish the daily cupboard. And the mattress factory south of downtown still claims "Sleep is Life." Passenger and freight trains clang through on the old tracks at two A.M. toward Del Rio, El Paso, Las Cruces—other places with lilting Spanish names. (*Do they wake you up? Are they our local lullaby?*)

The warehouses by the river have been turned into the Blue Star Arts Complex—galleries, studios, and loft-style rental units. Rumor is they have a waiting list. Although it's inspiring to see abandoned areas get lifted up like this, the heart of downtown itself shows signs of becoming a place for Temporary Visitors: knick-knack tourist stores, vendors of ugly T-shirts, pre-fab chain hotel/motels, and a Hard Rock Café have mushroomed as dozens of indigenous local businesses quietly disappeared. Where are all those honest, necessary places real residents used to go?

I miss the Post Office Café, the Stetson store, the elegant Frost Brothers department stores, the Kress dry-goods store in the spectacular art-deco building, the Alamo News Stand—I could go on and on and on. In pictures from the 1920s or 1940s of downtown San Antonio, the streets are crowded with honest daily bustle. I want to go inside these pictures and live in that other time. This city is rapidly losing what made it interesting to begin with. (*Are you noticing? Are you worried about it? When we talk about using specifics in writing, can we ignore these changes that surround us?*)

I wouldn't mind new things coming in, if it weren't at the expense of the old. If every storefront on Houston Street weren't abandoned now that everybody's at the sleek new downtown mall, I wouldn't mind the mall so much.

So what about it? I tell my writing classes that if we're noticing details, it's our job to document local losses, to examine them closely and to think about the precious, weird little details of our own neighborhoods. "Ah, miss," says Domingo, a student at David Crockett Elementary, "you want us to write about what changed over here, but you know it's much more interesting to write about what didn't change."

"Such as?"

"My mother. She never changes."

But Rico's seen Domingo's mother in a bad and good mood and he swears those moods were *different*. They argue awhile. Pleasantly. In the meantime I'm preparing everyone else for an "observation walk" out by Tarin's Meat Market on Zarzamora Street and the West Side Feed Store where they used to keep an angry monkey in a cage. We're heading out toward the gravel lots and the thirsty yards.

We will take pencils and papers. We'll tune in with our eyes and ears. We will not speak to one another—it's hard to observe closely if you're jabbering. I give them questions to consider in case they go blank. They write them down for reference. "What's right under my feet? What's so small I would have missed it if I weren't looking? What's quiet? What's pink? What's loud? Who's waiting for the bus? What does this smell remind me of?" We will make wild, flamboyant lists of things—the more specific, the better. We can *imagine* as well as record. "If you see a guy you never saw before, you can even make up a name for him. You can make up his story."

Somebody insists, "But ma'am, there's nothing out there! It's dullsville, ma'am!" Everybody laughs. But they like the idea that they're going outdoors to stretch their legs while other classes labor inside.

I read poems to get the class in a receptive mood, and we talk about the poems. "It's good to start scribbling already if a thought comes to you." I tell them they may write in Spanish, in English, or use a mixture of both languages, as many do when they talk. (Writing teachers must always be asking themselves: how can I make this link up to *their lives*, and *feel like home*?) I write some short poems on the board to focus on. (This is crucial. They need to *see poems* to be able to start *thinking poems*.)

Aquí

Mis pasos en esta calle
Resuenan
    en otra calle
donde
   oigo mis pasos
pasar en esta calle
donde

Sólo es real la niebla

   —Octavio Paz

Here

My steps along this street
resound
    in another street
in which
   I hear my steps
passing along this street
in which

Only the mist is real

    —Translated by Charles Tomlinson

("Ma'am , this guy is dreamy! I like how it's one street mixed up with another street. Do you think it's his memory echoing?")

Amanecer en Buenos Aires

Rompe la luz el azul celeste
Amanece en la Plaza San Martín
En cada flor hay esquirlas de cielo

   —José Emilio Pacheco

Dawn in Buenos Aires

Light breaks the celestial blue
It dawns in the Plaza San Martín

In every flower there are splinters of sky

—*Translated by Thomas Hoeksema*

Students invariably respond most warmly to connections—flower to sky, our town to Buenos Aires, or Guadalajara, or wherever. That's just *one* of the reasons why it's so important to use poems that come from other countries. I also love poems that link the little and the big.

Naranjada

Mañana partida,
los gajos de nubes
dejan caer su semilla.

La naranja de sol,
muda de ropa.

—*Luis Medina Gutiérrez*

Orangeade

At dawn
the cloud sections
drop their seeds.

The sunny orange
changes clothes.

—*Translated by Joan Darby Norris*

Canción de enero

La hora es fresca y los niños
  en la escuela con ansiedad aguardan
el perfil del carro de raspados:
  botellas de colores que confunden
con su cielo profundo la mirada.
  Soles, sueños del dulce principio...
el brillo de los rayos despierta
  en la nieve gris de los volcanes.

—*Alberto Blanco*

January Song

The hour is cool and from the school
children anxiously look for
the profile of the snow cone cart:
bottles of color that blend
long gazes with deep sky.
Suns, dreams of sweet origins . . .
the shine of the flash is born
on the gray volcano snow.

—Translated by Julio Marzán

Many times I read aloud sections of a poem too long to copy on the board and we talk about phrases and lines. I am careful to avoid the question "What does this mean?" which has been asked far too many times about poetry, as if words and images can't mean themselves, as if they were always tricking us. I prefer, "What does this make you see or wonder? Does this remind you of anything you know? Where does it take you?"

Hopefully it will remind them of what they are going to write.

I like the long poem "La plaza" by Antonio Deltoro of Mexico, a simple but rich listing of details found in a town's heart. The poem bounces comfortably from one line to the next, not making too much of anything, but using each item to create a sense of the whole. Here is the first third of the poem:

En la plaza
el asfalto descansa
toma vacaciones,
se vuelve pista de patinaje,
danzan las bicicletas,
beben los teporochos.

Hijos de papá,
con sus mamás,
salen de misa,

los gorriones, gorrones
disfrutan del festín
de las palomas:
pájaros de postín,
aves de cofia blanca.

El kiosko es un tíovivo
injertado en estatua,
un carrusel anquilosado

187

al que un día los caballitos
abandonaron.

La fuente en la plaza
es una palmera de agua,
la palmera una fuente;
la fuente y la palmera
son dos primas hermanas.

Las campanas de la iglesia
llaman a misa,
las del carrito de helados
mueven a risa.

The Plaza

In the plaza
the pavement has a rest,
takes a vacation,
becomes a skating rink,
bicycles dance,
the winos drink.

Daddy's children,
with their mamas,
come out of Mass,

the sparrows,
scroungers,
enjoy the pigeons' banquet;
swanky show-offs,
birds with white coifs.

The bandstand is a merry-go-round
grounded as a statue,
a carousel so old-fashioned
that one day the little horses
ran away.

The fountain in the plaza
is a palm tree of water,
the palm tree is a fountain;
the fountain and the palm tree
are two first cousins.

The church bells
call the people to Mass,
the bells on the ice cream cart
make the people laugh.

—*Translated by C. M. Mayo*

I suggest very basic techniques of listing (*Nouns! Remember nouns, my friends! It's not a "pretty" street or a "dull" street, but a street full of things!*)—detailing particular attributes ("a crooked blue fence" rather than just "a fence") and letting things bounce around inside us, creating responses ("The trees give us shade and what do we do for them? Nothing!" writes Maria E. Gutiérrez.)

I always feel I am evangelizing for the imagination in general, as all visiting writers must feel—we are meeting that wide-eyed "Aw come on!" with "Yes really! Let yourself go!" Sometimes I think the figurative, imaginative worlds have been so filtered out of young minds by now it's best to say "Yes yes yes" to any descriptive oddity.

So, after talking and reading and discussing and note-taking, all done with supersonic swiftness in approximately fifteen minutes, off we go into the streets for the next thirty.

I urge my students—whether elementary school age or adults—to work for "abundance" as they walk: Look hard, pick up the messages in the cracks you've stepped over every single morning. Later you can choose among your riches for your poem. You can polish later. Tonight you may take another walk closer to your house. We'll work on the poems during our next session, finding a few images or details we like best to center on. I tell them we're gathering clues—just keep asking, what makes our world out here different from any other world? My biggest "victory" comes when some guy who moaned and groaned about his dull neighborhood as we were starting out says, after weeks of walking and writing, "You know, I really changed my mind about this place! I mean, those old stoves over in Ramiro's uncle's yard are like, they all got *faces*, man! I feel like I could write ten poems about every single yard!"

In a town like San Antonio, the use of Spanish casts an even brighter light into the smiles. Even most English-speakers feel comfortable enough to pitch Spanish into our local talk, but there's an even greater interest triggered in inner-city classrooms when bilingual students feel *both* their languages are being welcomed or confirmed. Even if they decide to write only in English, it changes everything, I think. It says *yes* to all their words.

Here are some student poems:

En la calle de la luna

As I walk I sing of darkness, I sing of clouds,
how they change like people, they meet and they flee.
I sing of people, rainbow's light,
empty roads and wooded nights.
My voice is deep.
It sparkles to your ears
and swirls dust away.
My voice flaps and moves like a river.
It whispers to the world,
sometimes it shouts,
but always has a heart.
My voice can be a swan
and speak with its wings
but behind it is a shadow
that looks like the world.

       —Vangie Castillo, eighth grade

Mi calle

bright and shiny   straight and cracked
y clean sidewalks y picturas de animales
      y people
trees beside the sidewalks
hills y mountains
and the most importante
  is myself
great things around mi calle
street that leads to the city
tiendas y buildings
bonito gatitos around
    mi calle
y casas y perros y barkingful wonder
   buildings
   and houses
roosters around mi casa su casa
   who
  do you think

I
am am am
?

—Jesús Alarcón, Jr., first grade

My chicken lives in a silver ciudad.
Mi perro lives in a dusty doghouse.
Mi gato lives in an empty trashcan
   in the alley behind mi casa.
Mi hermano lives in a dream world.

—Ruben Hernandez, sixth grade

En mi ciudad Martians live in mobile homes.
In my city it rains and shines.
En mi ciudad it rains cats and dogs from the ground up.
In my city people go to restaurantes to eat.
People go to eat, and sleep in guitars.
En mi ciudad the teléfono rings y people answer it.
In my city people ring and phones answer us.

—Roland Morales, fourth grade

After seeing a young child gripping his mother's hand and rollerskating
carefully past us, Jamshid Afshar, a fifth grader, wrote this poem:

Rollerskate!

When I rollerskate
   I feel life in a way
   where time is as fast as I am.
When I rollerskate
   I feel power, like being
   superior to the world.
When I turn on my rollerskates
   it's like my life changing
   as I grow older.
When I rollerskate
   I feel that loneliness
   cannot catch me.

Bibliography

Blanco, Alberto. In *The Tree Is Older Than You Are*, edited by Naomi Shihab Nye. New York: Simon & Schuster, 1995. The translation of "Canción de enero" in that volume is by Judith Infante.

Deltoro, Antonio. In *The Tree Is Older Than You Are*, edited by Naomi Shihab Nye. New York: Simon & Schuster, 1995.

Gutierrez, Luis Medina. In *The Tree Is Older Than You Are*, edited by Naomi Shihab Nye. New York: Simon & Schuster, 1995.

Pacheco, José Emilio. *Selected Poems*, edited by George McWhirter in collaboration with the author. New York: New Directions, 1987.

Paz, Octavio. *Selected Poems*, edited by Eliot Weinberger. New York: New Directions, 1984.

MARK STATMAN

Reading and Seeing
Teaching Bilingual Calligrams

It is doubly enjoyable to teach calligrammatic poetry with a bilingual group. I like the play involved, the idea of the poem as something read *and* seen, and the movement between languages. The visual aspect—the sense that a poem's words, letters, and typeface, can be manipulated and arranged—enlarges our idea of what a poem can be, just as working in two languages enlarges our sense of language itself. The kids enjoy writing calligrams and don't seem to mind the amount of revision they often need to do to get their poems just right.

To introduce calligrams, I usually start with these two by Otto-Raúl Gonzáles (the translations are mine):

```
         olas              es           las                de
  Las        son     de    pu     y     alas      olas      pluma
         alas              ma                son


         olas              hilos        el                 reda
  Las        son     de    de     que   mar       en       a
         bolas             seda               des          solas


         waves             fo           the                of
  The        are     of    a      and   wings     waves     feathers
         wings             m                  are


         waves             threads      the                tan
  The        are     of    of     that  sea       un        gles
         balls             silk               each
```

Es un
misterio
de negro   gato que se
  color   duerme en el
    el   viejo sofa de
               la sala llena
                     de sombras y
                           recuerdos que mueven
                                       la
                                     cola

It is
a mystery
  colored   cat that
   black   sleeps on the
    the   old sofa in
               the parlor full
                     of shadows and
                           memories that move
                                       its
                                     tail

    I like these two poems for their simplicity of design and for their metaphoric transformations, the waves as wings, as balls of thread, the cat as a mystery. Before I give the poems to my students—usually second to sixth grade—I talk with them about metaphor and simile. We make up a bunch that I write on the board and save for making calligrams.

    Then I hand out the two Gonzáles poems. At first, the kids, especially the younger ones, are a little confused. They don't immediately see the waves and cat design, or how the waves can be wings of foam, or the wings waves of feathers. But I tell them to imagine that we're on a boat crossing the ocean. I begin to draw a stormy sea on the chalkboard, waves up and down, with the wing tips getting rougher and foamier, beginning to fly off the water's surface, higher and higher, as though they'd become the wings of birds. Or I suggest that sea birds had come down to the ocean, and were part of that roughness.

    The second metaphor of the first poem is easier to explain. We're at the seashore, looking out at the waves. A huge one is coming at us, but as it rolls in, it unrolls itself, like a ball of thread, so that by the time it arrives, there's just a single thread. Of course, this is an imprecise description, but the kids get the idea.

There's usually no problem explaining the cat poem. Why is the cat a mystery? Because it's part of the shadows, part of the dark room, almost invisible within the darkness. Also, because it has these memories. What are they? We can guess: hunting mice, being caught by a dog, eating, drinking, falling in love. But we can never know what a cat is really thinking and dreaming.

After we read and discuss the poems, I ask the students if they see anything odd about the way the poems appear. Since I've usually already taught the idea of the poetic line (I do this with third grade students and up), the kids have a sense of the importance of word arrangement. Sometimes, though, this knowledge of line actually prevents them from seeing the shape: they're looking for something more complex. Eventually, though, they see the waves, they see the cat's head. There's excitement at noticing that where it says "tail" *is* the tail.

We return to our group metaphors and similes on the board: "The sun is a gold watch ticking on top of the ocean. The moon shines in the sky like a silver dollar in my pocket. The trees are hair for the earth." I ask the kids to talk about possible shapes for each one. I use the image of pouring the words into a shape the way concrete can be poured to make a sidewalk. I remind them that although there are obvious shapes (a description of a flag has a flag shape, a description of a hand has a hand shape), sometimes the similes and metaphors can take on a number of different shapes, depending on what the author wants to emphasize. Should the poem take the shape of the sun, a clock, or the ocean? Should it be the moon or a coin? Hair, the earth, or a tree?

I recopy the metaphors and similes on the board into shapes suggested by the students. If colored chalk is available, I write in color where it seems appropriate (green on leaves, blue on ocean, etc).

Then I ask the kids to write their own poems. Pick an object, a person, or an idea and write a poem that describes it. I remind them to use similes and metaphors. I insist that they write a poem first—otherwise there's a tendency to forget that these are poems and not drawings.

Once the poems are written, I ask the students to experiment with a calligrammatic version. A lot of times, the poem is too long or too short to fit the shape and the students need to go back and revise the poem or revise their conception of the shape. Sometimes they get caught up in the direction of the writing (for example: writing a description of a cloud in the shape of the cloud might lead them into writing backwards). Or it isn't clear where the poem begins and ends. These are all things that students need to play with (emphasize the word *play*), until they arrive at a final version. If they want to use colors, I suggest they write the poems lightly in pencil and then go over them with markers or crayons (note to teachers: these make great bulletin board displays, and it's helpful to provide a regular printed version on the side if the poem seems too hard to decipher).

Here are two examples:

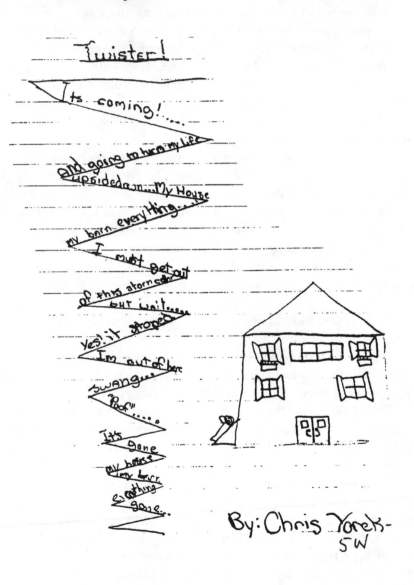

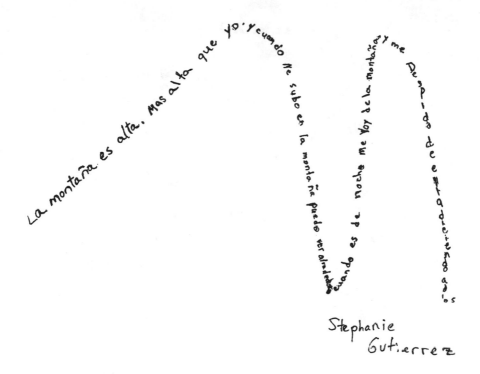

La montaña es alta. Mas alta que yo. Y cuando me subo en la montaña puedo ver alrededor. Cuando es de noche me voy de la montaña y me Despido de ella diciendo adios

Stephanie Gutierrez

Sometimes I give the kids more sophisticated models, such as the work of José Tablada. Tablada's sense of the connection between the verbal and the visual is striking. In "Luciernagas" ("Fireflies") he uses typography to fill the page with the light of the fireflies, the fullness of the garden, and the falling rain.

LUCIERNAGAS

La luz

de las

Luciérnagas

es un

blando   suspiro

Alternado

con **pausas**   de oscuridad

Pensamientos

sombríos   que se   disuelven

en gotas

instantáneas   de claridad

EL JARDIN ESTA LLENO

de suspiros de luz

Y por sus

frondas   escurriendo   van

como

lá

gri

mas   las últimas   gotas

De la

lluvia

lunar............

FIREFLIES

The light

        of the

                Fireflies

is a

        soft   **breath**

Alternating

        with **moments**   of darkness

Gloomy

    thoughts   **that**   **dissolve**

in **instantaneous**

      drops   of clarity

THE GARDEN IS FULL

      of breaths of light

And through its

      dripping   leaves   they go

like

   t

    ea

     rs   the last   **drops**

  of the

     lunar

       rain . . . .

—*Translated by Mark Statman*

The Blue Sky

The Blue Sky almost
    to
    blueness
    spreading
    all over

Clouds hanging
    from the dark blueness
    The
    sky
in
one
spot

      —Javier Moran, fifth grade

Snow falling
Like confetti
on New Year's
eve

Apple blossoms
falling
like snow on a
winter's day

    flowers
blooming like a rainbow
    on
    the
    field

bright stars
in the
sky
like eyes
in the audience

A clock ticking
like
someone's
heart
beating

    clouds
    in
    the
    sky
    like giant
    puffs of
    marshmallows

    —Jennifer Rivera, fifth grade

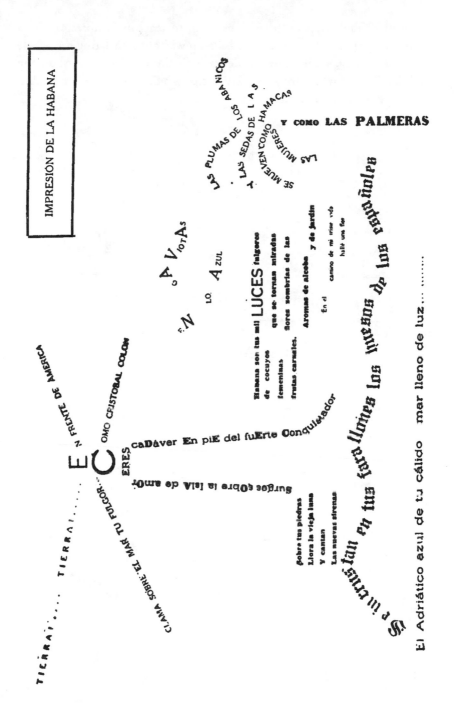

IMPRESIÓN DE LA HABANA

LAS PLUMAS DE LOS ABANICOS
Y LAS SEDAS DE LAS HAMACAS
SE MUEVEN COMO LAS MUJERES
Y COMO LAS **PALMERAS**

ᴺᵒ A VIOTAs
ᴺⁱ LO AZUL

LUCES fúlgores
Habana son tus mil
que se tornan miradas
de cocuyes
femeninas   flores sombrías de las
frutas carnales.
Aromas de alcoba   y de jardín
En el   camino de mi triste vida
halté una flor

COMO CRISTOBAL COLON
EN FRENTE DE AMÉRICA
C
ERES caDáver En piE del fuErte Conquistador
Surge ¿Sobre la IslA de amo?
Sobre tus piedras
Llora la vieja luna
y cantan
Las nuevas sirenas

TIERRA!.... TIERRA!....
CLAMA SOBRE EL MAR TU FULGOR

Se incrustan en tus faros llenos los huesos de los españoles

El Adriático azul de tu cálido   mar lleno de luz.... ....

Another Tablada poem that is exciting to teach is "Impresión de la Habana." The entire scene is all words. Even without translating the whole poem completely, I can show students how the lighthouse is shouting "land, land," that where they see a palm tree is a description of that palm, where they see water is a description of the sea.

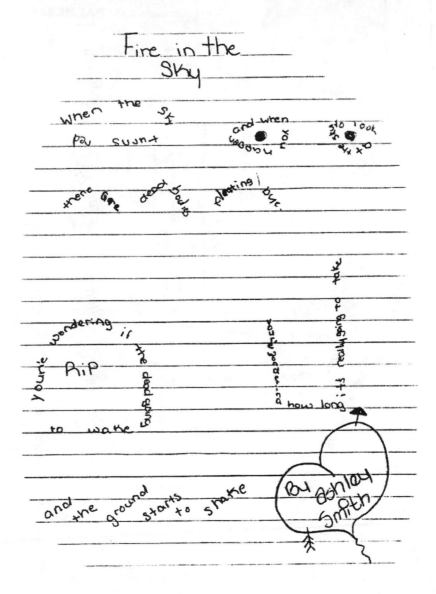

After we've spent time "reading" the poem, I ask them to think about a place they'd like to describe and then to write a poem describing it. I remind them to use details in their descriptions, paying attention to all the things we would be able to see and hear there. Once they've written that poem, they can think about how to turn it into a calligram.

Tablada's Havana calligram can serve as a model for larger poetic collaborations. For several years at the Daniel Webster Magnet Arts and Science School in New Rochelle, N.Y., during the school's lengthy studio arts program, we were able to create a number of calligrammatic murals. The students worked in groups. Each group chose a setting (place and time) and figured out all the different things they wanted to write about in that setting. Individual students became responsible for writing individual calligrams for these things. After all the poems were written, the students took their smaller concrete poems and figured out how to arrange them (we used a number of surfaces, including wood, foam core board and heavy brown paper). Poems were then either written on the surface or attached with glue. Although the results no longer hang on the school's walls (they did so for several years, each year more and more being added), even to describe them now invites one to imagine what they must have been in all their linguistic, color, and design glory. A mural about a city street, for example, had a calligram of a 4th of July brass band marching on a poem about a street while a calligrammed hot dog vendor hawked calligrammatic hot dogs to calligrammatic people who were wandering in and out of calligrammatic shops. A calligrammatic mural about the ocean had a calligrammatic boat floating on top of calligrammatic waves under which swam calligrammatic fish, whales, and submarines. Above it all, shining brightly, a calligrammatic sun with calligrammatic seagulls flying through the air.

Bibliography

Gonzáles, Otto-Raúl. In *República de poetas*, edited by Sergio Mondragón. Mexico City: Martín Casillas Editores, 1985.

Tablada, José Juan. *Obras*. Vol. 1. Mexico City: Centro de Estudios Literarios, Universidad Nacional Autónoma de México, 1971.

Other Models

The range of Latino literature and of poetry in Spanish is wider than is often thought. The following poems provide useful models that give some idea of that range.

∾ ∾ ∾

Nicanor Parra

Chilean poet Nicanor Parra (b. 1914) uses the roller coaster as a metaphor for his own poetry:

Montaña rusa

Durante medio siglo
La poesía fue
El paraíso del tonto solemne.
Hasta que vine yo
Y me instalé con mi montaña rusa.

Suban, si les parece.
Claro que yo no respondo si bajan
Echando sangre por boca y narices.

—Nicanor Parra

Roller Coaster

For half a century
poetry was
the paradise of the solemn fool.
Until I came along
and moved in with my roller coaster.

Get on, if you want to.
Clearly it's not my fault if you come down
spurting blood from your mouth and nostrils.

—Translated by Ron Padgett

Parra is a master of an ironic and playful naughtiness. The structure of this poem is simple: in the first stanza he brags, and in the second he issues a warning. After translating this poem into English, a small group of bilingual elementary school students came up with this poem:

La poesía del fregadero

Yo soy muy bueno lavando los platos.
El fregadero se parece come humo y arena movediza.
¡No entren! ¡Es peligroso!

The Poem of the Sink

I'm very good at washing the dishes.
The sink looks like smoke and quicksand.
Keep out! Danger!

—*Bilingual class, P.S. 19, New York*

Older students might also enjoy Parra's "The Teachers," which begins:

Los profesores nos volvieron locos
a preguntas que no venían al caso
cómo se suman números complejos
hay o no hay arañas en la luna
cómo murió la familia del zar
¿es posible cantar con la boca cerrada?
quién le pintó bigotes al la Gioconda
cómo se llaman los habitantes de Jerusalén
hay o no hay oxígeno en el aire
cuántos son los apóstoles de Cristo
cuál es el significado de la palabra consueta
cuáles fueron las palabras que dijo Cristo el la cruz
quién es el autor de Madame Bovary

In William Jay Smith's translation:

Our teachers drove us nuts
with their irrelevant questions:
how do you add compound numbers
are there or are there not spiders on the moon
how did the family of the czar die
can one sing with one's mouth shut
who painted the mustache on the Mona Lisa
what are the inhabitants of Jerusalem called

is there or is there not oxygen in the air
how many apostles did Christ have
what is the meaning of "consubstantial"
what were the words Christ spoke on the cross
who is the author of *Madame Bovary*

Parra goes on with this list, interspersing descriptions of his teachers and his bad attitude as a student. The ironic thing is that the poem suggests that he was actually quite a good student.

≈ ≈ ≈

Vicente Huidobro

Vicente Huidobro (1893–1948) was influenced by the modern art and poetry he encountered when he lived in Paris around the time of the First World War. In the fifth canto of his long poem *Altazor*, he mentions a windmill, which sets him off on a list that begins:

Molino de viento
Molino de aliento
Molino de cuento
Molino de intento
Molino de aumento
Molino de ungüento
Molino de sustento
Molino de tormento
Molino de salvamento

Mill of wind
Mill of breath
Mill of story
Mill of purpose
Mill of growth
Mill of ointment
Mill of food
Mill of torture
Mill of safety

—*Translated by Stephen Fredman*

In a Rabelaisian mood, Huidobro continues this list, with variations of the preposition, for another 180 lines!

He also uses the list form in the following, somewhat surrealistic poem:

Fuerzas naturales

Una mirada
$\qquad$ para abatir al albatros

Dos miradas
$\qquad$ para detener el paisaje
$\qquad$ al borde del río

Tres miradas
$\qquad$ para cambiar la niña en
$\qquad$ volantín

Cuatro miradas
$\qquad$ para sujetar el tren que
$\qquad\qquad\qquad$ cae en abismo

Cinco miradas
$\qquad$ para volver a encender las estrellas
$\qquad$ apagadas por el huracán

Seis miradas
$\qquad$ para impedir el nacimiento
$\qquad$ del niño acuático

Siete miradas
$\qquad$ para prolongar la vida de
$\qquad$ la novia

Ocho miradas
$\qquad$ para cambiar el mar
$\qquad$ en cielo

Nueve miradas
$\qquad$ para hacer bailar los
$\qquad$ árboles del bosque

Diez miradas
$\qquad$ para ver la belleza que se presenta
$\qquad$ entre sueño y una catástrofe

Natural Forces

One glance
$\qquad$ to knock down the albatross

Two glances
$\qquad$ to stop the landscape
$\qquad$ at the river's edge

Three glances
$\qquad$ to change the girl into
$\qquad$ a kite

Four glances

> to hold back the train which
> falls in the chasm

Five glances

> to relight the stars
> blown out by the hurricane

Six glances

> to prevent the birth
> of the acquatic child

Seven glances

> to prolong the life of
> the bride

Eight glances

> to change the sea
> into sky

Nine glances

> to make the trees in the wood
> dance

Ten glances

> to see the beauty that is present
> between a dream and a catastrophe

—Translated by David Ossman and Carlos Hagen

≈ ≈ ≈

Frank Lima

New York Poet Frank Lima (b. 1939) wrote the following poem in his early
twenties, about the death of boxer Benny Paret in the ring. Sounding the
ringside bell twelve times is a boxing ritual to commemorate the deceased.

The Memory of Benny (Kid) Paret

1

Twelve Bells
    Benny's on the ropes
Twelve Bells
    he has no feet
Twelve Bells
    he can't make gloves
Twelve Bells
    one rope through his head

Twelve Bells
    one rope through his chest
Twelve Bells
    one rope through his leg
Twelve Bells
    a black pig on three spits
Twelve Bells
    a rubber apple in his mouth
Twelve Bells
    his jaw hangs like a moth
Twelve Bells
    his face is a torn flower
Twelve Bells
    his hands fall off the clocks
Twelve Bells
    he's a fly in a glass of milk.

        2
Little Benny's tears
        wounded pebbles on the
            coffin lids
    your folded hands
        two dead countries
          in my head
   the rope burns
     cold welts on your back
  your head is a turban
         of bandages
  your eyes are bread
     I can't eat
  the ring is a crib
      where you sleep
Benny's an empty bag.

You might want to have your students choose a momentous instant, and then "freeze" it the way Lima does. You might also present this poem alongside Lorca's "Lament for Ignacio Sánchez Mejía," an elegy for a dead bullfighter, with its refrain of "At five in the afternoon."

Readers should also see Lima's collection *Underground with the Oriole*.

≈ ≈ ≈

Victor Hernández Cruz

Born in Puerto Rico and raised in New York, Victor Hernández Cruz (b. 1949) is a highly inventive and often witty poet who writes English poems, Spanish poems, and bilingual poems. His first book, *Snaps*, published when Cruz was nineteen, is filled with the musicality of Cruz's neighborhood and culture. The following poem is from *Snaps*:

going uptown to visit miriam

on the train
old ladies playing football
going for empty seats

very funny persons

the train riders
                 are silly people
                 I am a train rider

but no one knows where i am
going to take this train

to take this train
to take this train

the ladies   read popular
paperbacks   because they
are popular   they get off
at 42 to change for the
westside line   or off
59 for the department store

the train pulls in & out
the white walls   darkness   white walls   darkness

ladies looking up   I
wonder where they going
the dentist   pick up
husband pick up wife
pick up kids
pick up ?grass?
to library   to museum
to laundromat   to school

but no one knows where i am
going to take this train

to take this train

to visit miriam
to visit miriam

& to kiss her
on the cheek
& hope i don't
see sonia on the
street

But no one knows where i'm taking
this train
      taking this train
      to visit miriam.

Adolescents like this poem for many reasons: the clarity and simplicity of its language, its humor, its romance, the speaker's distance from the adult world, and the drama of having a secret. After reading and hearing this poem, students could write about a moment in which they are aware of the sharp border between their internal and external experiences.

Other books by Cruz include *Mainland; Tropicalization; By Lingual Wholes; Rhythm, Content and Flavor;* and *Red Beans.*

≈ ≈ ≈

Gabriela Mistral

This poem by the Chilean Nobel laureate introduces the power of the symbol, an object (or image) that embodies a complex structure of ideas that could be difficult to express in words. In this instance, bread symbolizes a union with the whole world, basic human needs, the cycles of cultivation and harvest, the history of humanity. Have your students think of a single thing that can contain or suggest many feelings or pictures. If this poem is a bit long for younger students, excerpt the first five stanzas, which retain the essential idea of the symbol.

Pan

Dejaron un pan en la mesa,
mitad quemado, mitad blanco,

pellizcado encima y abierto
en unos migajones de ampo.

Me parece nuevo o como no visto,
y otra cosa que él no me ha alimentado,
pero volteando su miga, sonámbula,
tacto y olor se me olvidaron.

Huele a mi madre cuando dio su leche,
huele a tres valles por donde he pasado:
a Aconagua, a Pátzcuaro, a Elqui,
y a mis entrañas cuando yo canto.

Otros olores no hay en la estancia
y por eso él así me ha llamado;
y no hay nadie tampoco en la casa
sino este pan abierto en un plato,
que con su cuerpo me reconoce
y con el mío yo reconozco.

Se ha comido en todos los climas
el mismo pan en cien hermanos:
pan de Coquimbo, pan de Oaxaca,
pan de Santa Ana y de Santiago.

En mis infancias yo le sabía
forma de sol, de pez o de halo,
y sabía mi mano su miga
y el calor de pichón emplumado . . .

Después le olvidé hasta este día
en que los dos nos encontramos,
yo con mi cuerpo de Sara vieja
y él con el suyo de cinco años.

Amigos muertos con que comíalo
en otras valles sientan el vaho
de un pan en septiembre molido
y en agosto en Castilla segado.

Es otro y es el que comimos
en tierras donde se acostaron.
Abro la miga y les doy su calor;
lo volteo y les pongo su hálito.

La mano tengo de él rebosada
y la mirada puesta en mi mano;
entrego un llanto arrepentido
por el olvido de tantos años,
y la cara se me envejece
y me renace en este hallazgo.

Como se halla vacía la casa,
estemos juntos los reecontrados,
sobre este mesa sin carne y fruta,
los dos es este silencio humano,
hasta que seamos otra vez uno
y nuestro día haya acabado . . .

Bread

They've left a loaf of bread
out on the table—half-burnt, half white,
pinched on top and open,
a few snowy crumbs.

It looks fresh, as if
no one had looked at it yet,
and only bread has nourished me.
But turning a piece in my fingers, I drift off,
forget how it feels and smells.

And I can smell my mother's milk,
Aconagua, Pátzcuaro, Elqui,
the three valleys I've passed through,
and my insides when I sing.

Other odors aren't in the room,
it's the bread that calls me.
No one in the house
except for this loaf on a plate
that knows me with its body
as I know it with mine.

In every land they eat this,
the same bread in a hundred brothers:
Coquimbo bread, Oaxaca bread,
the bread of Santiago, Santa Ana.

As a child I knew it
shaped like a sun, fish, or halo;
my hands knew its crumbs,
warm as a young pigeon.

Then I forgot it, until today
we found ourselves together,
my body old as Sarah's
next to a five-year-old child.

Dead friends I've eaten with
in other valleys: feel the mist
of a bread ground in September,
reaped in the August of Castille.

It's a different bread, and the same
we ate together, in the lands
where they lay down to die.
I break the piece, give them its warmth;
turn it in my fingers,
offer them a breath.

My hand is filled with bread,
my gaze is on my hand.
I break into tears, sorry
for forgetting whole years, and my face
grows old on me, or is reborn
in this discovery.

Since the house is empty,
let us, the reencountered, be together
at this table without meat or fruit,
the two of us
in a human silence,
until our day has ended
and we're one again.

—Translated by Marti Moody

≈ ≈ ≈

Martín Espada

Martín Espada's poem "Tiburón" ("Shark") is reminiscent of the Guatemalan Miguel Angel Asturias's discussion of how Native Americans turn daily reality into myth: a garbage truck becomes a hungry monster. Have your students turn reality into magic by describing things seen every day, as Espada describes the shark.

Tiburón

East 116th
and a long red car
stalled with the hood up
roaring salsa
like a prize shark
mouth yanked open
and down into the stomach
the radio
of the last fisherman
still tuned
to his lucky station

≈ ≈ ≈

Ana Castillo

The poet Ana Castillo uses the images of silence and sound in diverse ways in "A Marriage of Mutes." The poem can be used to encourage students to write in their own images the different ways that people say things, even without words or sounds.

A Marriage of Mutes

In the house
that was his house
where the woman who lived there
cut the vegetables
hacked the chicken
boiled on the stove
and waited across the table
as he ate, with eyes that asked
Was it all right? Was it enough?—
the woman who slept with him
changed the linen
scrubbed oil from his coveralls
hung laundry on the line
never sought the face of the woman
across the yard who hung sheets,
coveralls and underwear—

in the house where this man lived
so at peace with himself
the air grew sparse one morning.

The hall to the bathroom narrowed
as his feet grew angular and
head lightened.
He startled himself to hear his first
"caw"—beating black wings against walls,
knocking down picture frames of the woman's
ancestors, the offspring's bronzed shoes
off the buffet.
One could only guess what he might
have said had his beak contained teeth.
The woman who always anticipated
his needs opened a window.
She would have wanted the crow to sit
on the couch
to read with her,
listen to music,
languish in a moment of peace
before the bird who was the man
she had lived with in such gratitude flew off,
but of course, it was too much to ask.

It had always been too much to ask.

≈ ≈ ≈

Nancy Morejón

The Cuban Nancy Morejón's "In the Streetcars' Shade" offers an interesting exercise for students to write about relatives they have never seen.

A la sombra de los tranvías
para Eliseo Diego

A la sombra de los tranvías,
abuela, ¿traia recogida una trenza
o era el relato familiar
quien lo afirmaba?
Mi pobre abuela . . . que nunca vi.

In the Streetcars' Shade
for Eliseo Diego

In the streetcars' shade . . .
grandmother, did she wear her hair
braided, or was that just
the family tale?
My poor grandmother . . . whom I never saw.

  —Translated by H. R. Hays

≈ ≈ ≈

César Vallejo

In "The Spider," César Vallejo (1895–1938) reiterates those circumstances of life ("little deaths") that remind us of our limitations. Here is a spider, a "traveler" with so many legs, unable to escape his predicament. Ask your students if they can think of a situation that, despite appearances, can't be remedied: a big strong man who can't keep from crying if he's reminded of something sad. This poem pressents an opportunity to discuss symbol, metaphor, and irony. Your students can also talk about whether or not they can identify with this insect, and how it feels. Imitating Vallejo, the students can write about a thing or animal (not people) they normally dislike, but placing it in situations that cause them to sympathize with it. Have the poems describe both the unlikeable and the sympathetic sides of the thing or animal.

La Araña

  Es una araña enorme que ya no anda;
una araña incolora, cuyo cuerpo,
una cabeza y un abdomen, sangra.

  Hoy la he visto de cerca. Y con qué esfuerzo
hacia todos los flancos
sus pies innumerables alargaba.
Y he pensado en sus ojos invisibles,
los pilotos fatales de la araña.

  Es una araña que temblaba fija
en un filo de piedra;
el abdomen a un lado,
y al otro la cabeza.

Con tantos pies la pobre, y aún no puede
resolverse. Y, al verla
atónita en tal trance,
hoy me ha dado qué pena esa viajera.

Es una araña enorme, a quien impide
el abdomen seguir a la cabeza.
Y he pensado en sus ojos
y en sus pies numerosos.
¡Y me ha dado qué pena esa viajera!

The Spider

It is an enormous spider that no longer moves;
A colorless spider, whose body,
A head and an abdomen, is bleeding.

Today I have seen it from close by. And with what efforts
Toward all sides
It was stretching its innumerable feet!
I thought of its invisible eyes,
The spider's fatal pilots.

It is a spider that quivered, caught
On the edge of a stone,
The abdomen on one side,
The head on the other.

Poor thing with so many feet and still it cannot
Find a solution. And, seeing it
Stupefied in such an emergency,
How I am troubled today by that traveller!

It is an enormous spider, whose abdomen
Keeps it from following its head.
And I thought of its eyes
And its numerous feet.
And how I am troubled by that traveller!

—*Translated by H. R. Hays*

≈ ≈ ≈

Vicente Aleixandre

Vicente Aleixandre's "To My Dog" is a poem of address that subtly reverses the roles (as signaled in line 2), so that the reader isn't alwats sure if it's the poet addressing the dog or the dog addressing the poet, or a combination of the two, all of which is an expression of the poet's desire to be "down where [the dog] lives" in order to find a higher life form, one beyond language, "of serenity and silence."

A mi perro

Oh, sí, lo sé, buen "Sirio", cuando me miras con tus grandes ojos profundos,
Yo bajo adonde tú estas
y en tu reino me mezclo contigo, buen "Sirio", buen perro mío, y me salvo
  contigo.
Aquí en tu reino de serenidad y silencio, donde la voz humana nunca se oye,
converso en el oscurecer y entro profundamente en tu mediodía.
Tú me has conducido a tu habitacíon, donde existe el tiempo que nunca se
  pone.
Un presente continuo preside nuesto diálogo, en el que el hablar es el tuyo tan
  sólo.
Yo callo y mudo te contemplo, y me yergo y te miro. Oh, cuán profundos ojos
  conocedores.
Pero no puedo decirte nada, aunque tú me comprendes . . . Oh, yo te escucho.
Allí oigo tu ronco decir y saber desde el mismo centro infinito de tu presente.
Tus largas orejas suavísimas, tu cuerpo de soberanía y de fuerza,
tu ruda pezuña peluda que toca la materia del mundo,
el arco de tu aparicíon y esos hondos ojos apaciguados
donde la Creacíon jamás irrumpió como una sorpresa.
Allí, en tu cueva, en tu averno donde todo es cenit, te entendí, aunque no
  pude hablarte.
Todo era fiesta en mi corazón, que saltaba en tu derredor, mientras tú eras tu
  mirar entendiéndome.
Desde mi sucederse y mi consumirse te veo, un instante parado a tu vera,
pretendiendo quedarme y reconocerme.
Pero yo pasé, transcurrí y tú, oh gran perro mío, persistes.
Residido en tu luz, inmóvil en tu seguridad, no pudiste más que entenderme.
Y yo salí de tu cueva y descendí a mi alvéolo viajador, y, al volver la cabeza, en
  la linde
vi, no sé, algo como unos ojos misericordes.

To My Dog

Yes, it's clear to me, good Sirius, whenever you look at me with your big,
    thoughtful eyes.
I come down here where you live—or I come up—
and join you in your kingdom where you save me, my good dog Sirius.
Here in your calm and quiet world where there are no human voices
I chat with you in the evening; I go straight to the middle of your day.
You've brought me to your home where there's a kind of time that has no
    sunsets.
At unending present stands over our conversation. You're the only one who
    talks,
I fall silent and look at you as if I'd lost my voice. I sit up and watch. Your eyes
    are so thoughtful and wise!
But even though you'd understand, there's nothing for me to say. . . . I just
    listen.
I hear your hoarse speech and wisdom rise from the soundless core of the
    present.
Your long, incredibly soft ears, your strong proud body,
your rough shaggy paws in touch with the material world,
the curve of your silhouette and those calm, unfathomed eyes
where the Creation never breaks in to upset you.
There in your cave, in your dark hole full of light, I knew what you meant
    though I couldn't speak.
My heart swelled with joy and went bounding around you (while you kept
    giving me that knowing look).
From my expansion and exhaustion I can see you, pausing a moment at your
    side,
trying to stop me and figure me out.
But I kept going, I went on while you stayed, my big friend.
You live in your own light, your security doesn't change, the best you could do
    for me was understand.
And I left your cave and went down to my little traveler's compartment. And
    when I turned my head at the border
I could see—what was it?—something like the eyes of pardon.

   —*Translated by Lewis Hyde*

This poem is a good example of irony, which the teacher can discuss before
inviting students to imagine other relationships in which their assumptions proved to be wrong. Younger students could be reminded of a similar
use of (dramatic) irony in the film *Toy Story*, in which the toys, so unexpect-
edly human, have feelings that their owner never imagined. In Aleixandre's

poem, the dog is the teacher. He understands the poet, who "listens" to his dog's wise silence, respecting his intelligent gaze.

≈ ≈ ≈

Julio Marzán

The Carousel Boy

Carousel breeze, glee and gliding,
Carousel boy, dipping and rising,
His unfettered head
Helium on a thread,
His hand waving
To no one behind us.

Slant-eyed boy, dipping and rising,
In factory clothes, glee and gliding,
On Carousel wings,
The old drum pounding,
His smile stretching
For no one behind us.

We mounted Arabians, glee and gliding,
Manes in the wind, dipping and rising,
The Carousel's kingdom
Whirling around us,
Thousands of people
Waving and shouting.

Is the subject really a boy? Why is he slant-eyed? Is it the carousel or a particular condition that makes him smile and seem funny to us? He may seem boy-like and odd and even silly because he's seeing things that others don't see. But once we enter the magic, spinning world of the carousel, we too are made happy and perhaps seem silly to others looking at us. Students can write a poem about someone who sees things his or her friends don't see, or a poem about someone who is "different." The poem's use of an upbeat rhythm offers a good opportunity for a discussion of the use of rhythm, either as way to reinforce a poem's content or to go against its grain.

Bibliography

Aleixandre, Vicente. *A Longing for the Light: Selected Poems.* Edited by Lewis Hyde. New York: Harper & Row, 1979.

Castillo, Ana. *My Father Was a Toltec.* New York: W. W. Norton, 1995.

Cruz, Victor Hernández. *Snaps.* New York: Random House, 1969.

Espada, Martín. *Trumpets from the Island of Their Eviction.* Tempe, Ariz.: Bilingual Review Press, 1987.

Huidobro, Vicente. *The Selected Poetry of Vicente Huidobro.* Edited by David M. Guss. New York: New Directions, 1981.

Lima, Frank. *Inventory.* New York: Tibor de Nagy Editions, 1964.

Marzán, Julio. *Translations without Originals.* Berkeley, Calif.: I. Reed Books, 1986.

Mistral, Gabriela. In *Open to the Sun,* edited by Nora Jacquez Wieser. Van Nuys, Calif.: Perivale Press, 1979.

Morejón, Nancy. *Where the Island Sleeps Like a Wing: Selected Poetry.* Translated by Kathleen Weaver. Oakland, Calif.: The Black Scholar Press, 1985.

Parra, Nicanor. *Antipoems: New and Selected.* Edited by David Unger. New York: New Directions, 1985.

Vallejo, César. In *12 Spanish American Poets,* edited by H. R. Hays. Boston: Beacon Press, 1972.

Bibliography and Other Resources

BOOKS

Aparicio, Frances R., ed. *Latino Voices.* Brookfield, Ct.: Millbrook Press, 1994. An anthology of fiction, nonfiction, and poetry for young adult readers.

Ardjis, Homero. "Hay silencio . . . / There's silence" in *Un ojo en el muro / An Eye in the Wall.* Santa Fe, N.M.: Tooth of Time Books, 1986.

————. Exaltation of Light. Eliot Weinberger, trans. and ed. Brockport, N.Y.: BOA Editions, 1981.

Aristotle. *Rhetoric* and *Poetics. Rhetoric* translated by W. Rhys Roberts. *Poetics* translated by Ingram Bywater. Introduction by Friedrich Solmsen. New York: The Modern Library, 1954.

Augenbraum, Harold; Terry Quinn; and Ilan Stavans, eds. *Bendíceme, América: Latino Writers of the United States.* New York: Mercantile Library, 1993. Nine talks on U.S. Latino fiction.

Augenbraum, Harold. *Latinos in English: A Selected Bibliography of Latino Fiction Writers of the United States.* New York: The Mercantile Library, 1992.

Blanco, Alberto. *Dawn of the Senses: Selected Poems.* Juvenal Acosta, ed.

————. In *The Tree Is Older Than You Are,* edited by Naomi Shihab Nye. New York: Simon & Schuster, 1995.

Brotchie, Alastair, compiler. *A Book of Surrealist Games.* Edited by Mel Gooding. Translations by Alexis Lykiard and Jennifer Batchelor. Boston & London: Shambhala Redstone Editions, 1995.

Cardenal, Ernesto. *Epigramas.* Boulder, Colo.: Lodestar Press, DATE?

————. "En el lago de Nicaragua" in *Antologia de la poesia hispano-americano.* Madrid: Selecciones Austral/Espasa Calipe, 1984.

Cardona, Rodolfo. *Ramón: A Study of Gómez de la Serna and His Works .* New York: Eliseo Torres & Sons, 1957.

Castillo, Otto Rene. *Tomorrow Triumphant.* San Francisco: Night Horn Books, 1984.

Cisneros, Sandra. *The House on Mango Street.* New York: Vintage Books, 1989.

Carlson, Lori, ed. *Cool Salsa: Bilingual Poems on Growing Up Latino in the United States.* New York: Henry Holt & Co., 1994.

Clement, Jennifer. *El Próximo extrano / The Next Stranger.* Mexico City: Ediciones el Tucan de Virginia, 1993.

Cruz, Victor Hernández; Quintana, Leroy V.; and Suarez, Virgil, eds. *Paper Dance: 55 Latino Poets.* New York: Persea Books, 1995.

Deltoro, Antonio. In *The Tree Is Older Than You Are,* edited by Naomi Shihab Nye. New York: Simon & Schuster, 1995.

Durán, Cheli, ed. *The Yellow Canary Whose Eye Is So Black.* New York: Macmillan, 1977.

Ellowitch, Azi. *Hidden Treasures: An Annotated Bibliography of Puerto Rican, Nuyorican, and Caribbean Literature for Use in Adult Basic Education.* Bronx, N.Y.: Institute for Literacy Studies, Lehman College, 1991.

Gardiol, Rita (Mazzetti). *Ramón Gómez de la Serna.* New York: Twayne Publishers, Inc. / Twayne World Authors Series No. 338, 1974.

Gibbons, Reginald, ed. *New Writing from Mexico.* Evanston, Ill.: Triquarterly Books, Northwestern University, 1992.

Gómez de la Serna, Ramón. *Total de greguerías.* Madrid: Aguilar, 1962.

———. *Greguerías (Selección).* Selection and introduction by Gaspar Gómez de la Serna. Salamanca: Ediciones Anaya, 1969. A paperback selection of *greguerías.*

———. *Dalí.* New York: William Morrow and Company, Inc., 1979. Translated from the Spanish by Nicholas Fry; other essays translated from the Italian by Elisabeth Evans. Ramón's unfinished essay (25 pages) as well as essays by others on Gómez de la Serna and Dalí, a Dalí chronology, illustrations of 68 works by Dalí, and other materials.

————. *Some Greguerías.* Translated by Helen Granville-Barker. New York: n.p., but "Printed by William E. Rudge's Sons" appears on final page, 1944.

————. *Greguerías: The Wit and Wisdom of Ramón Gómez de la Serna.* Selected, introduced, and translated by Philip Ward. Cambridge, England, and New York: The Oleander Press, 1982.

————. *Movieland.* Translated from the Spanish by Angel Flores. New York: The Macaulay Company, 1930.

————. *The Gentleman with "It."* New York: The American Guild, n.d. One wonders if indeed this book, cited in bibliographies, was ever published at all.

————. *Aphorisms.* Selected, translatedand introduced by Miguel Gonzalez-Gerth. Pittsburgh, Pa.: Latin American Literary Review Press / Series: Discoveries, 1989. A quite good translation of selected *greguerías.*

Gonzáles, Otto-Raúl. In *República de poetas*, edited by Sergio Mondragón. Mexico City: Martín Casillas Editores, 1985.

Guillén, Nicolás. *Sóngoro cosongo.* Buenos Aires: Editorial Losada, 1952.

Gutierrez, Luis Medina. In *The Tree Is Older Than You Are*, edited by Naomi Shihab Nye. New York: Simon & Schuster, 1995.

Hernández, Miguel. *Miguel Hernández and Blas de Otero: Selected Poems*, edited by Timothy Baland and Hardie St. Martin. Boston: Beacon Press, 1972.

Jiménez, Mayra. "Ayer" in *Cuando poeta.* Heredia, Costa Rica: Editorial de la Universidad Nacional.

Jordan, Martha Black. *Manos en agua / Hands in Water.* Mexico City: Ediciones el Tucan de Virginia, 1994.

Koch, Kenneth, and Kate Farrell. *Sleeping on the Wing.* New York: Vintage Books, 1981.

Lorca, Federico García. *Canciones y poemas para niños.* San Juan, Puerto Rico: Editorial Labor, 1993.

————. *Antología poética.* Selected by Guillermo de Torre and Rafael Alberti. Buenos Aires: Editorial Losada, 1957.

————. *Selected Poems of García Lorca.* Francisco García Lorca and Donald Allen, eds. New York: New Directions, 1955.

Machado, Antonio. *Poesías.* Buenos Aires: Losada, 1943.

Marzán, Julio, ed. *Inventing a Word: An Anthology of Twentieth-Century Puerto Rican Poetry.* New York: Columbia University Press, 1980.

Muñoz, David. In *Tonantzin.* San Antonio, Texas: Guadalupe Cultural Arts Center. March 1985 issue.

Morejón, Nancy. *Where the Island Sleeps Like a Wing.* Oakland, Calif.: Black Scholar Press, 1985.

Neruda, Pablo. *The Book of Questions.* Trans. William O'Daly. Port Townsend, Wash.: Copper Canyon Press, 1991.

————. *The Captain's Verses (Los Versos del Capitán).* Donald D. Walsh, ed. New York: New Directions, 1972.

————. *Stones of the Sky.* Port Townsend, Wash.: Copper Canyon Press, 1987.

————. "The Word." *In Lives on the Line: The Testimony of Contemporary Latin American Authors.* Doris Meyer, ed. Berkeley: University of California Press, 1988.

————. *Late and Posthumous Poems, 1968–1974.* Edited and translated by Ben Belitt. Bilingual edition. New York: Grove Weidenfeld, 1988.

————. *Selected Odes of Pablo Neruda.* Trans. Margaret Sayers Peden. Berkeley, Calif: Univ. of California Press, 1990.

————. *Neruda and Vallejo: Selected Poems.* Trans. Robert Bly and James Wright. Boston, Mass.: Beacon, 1971.

Nye, Naomi Shihab. *The Tree Is Older Than You Are.* New York: Simon & Schuster, 1995.

Ortega, Julio, and Ewing Campbell, eds. *The Plaza of Encounters.* Austin, Tex.: Latitudes Press, 1981.

Oliphant, Dave, and Luis Ramos-García, eds. *Washing the Cow's Skull / Lavando la calavera de vaca.* Cedar Park, Tex.: Prickly Pear Press, 1981.

Pacheco, José Emilio. *Selected Poems*, edited by George McWhirter in collaboration with the author. New York: New Directions, 1987.

Paz, Octavio. *Selected Poems*, edited by Eliot Weinberger. New York: New Directions, 1984.

Soto, Gary. *A Fire in My Hands*. New York: Scholastic, 1990.

Tablada, José Juan. *Obras*. Vol. 1. Mexico City: Centro de Estudios Literarios, Universidad Nacional Autónoma de México, 1971.

Tramontane Group, eds. *Ruido de sueños / Noise of Dreams*. Mexico City: Ediciones el Tucan de Virginia, 1994.

Zaid, Gabriel, ed. *Omnibus de poésia mexicana*. Mexico City: Siglo Veintiuno Editores, 1991.

Zavatsky, Bill. "Metaphor," in *The Teachers & Writers Handbook of Poetic Forms*. Edited by Ron Padgett. New York: Teachers and Writers Collaborative, 1987.

Note: For additional resources, see the annotated bibliography following John Oliver Simon's essay in this volume.

PUBLISHERS

Arte Publico is the largest publisher of Latino literature in America. To obtain their catalogs of adult, young adult, and children's books, write to Arte Público Press, University of Houston, 4800 Calhoun, Houston, TX 77204-2090, or call 800-633 ARTE.

Curbstone Press publishes contemporary writing from Latin America and Latino communities in the U.S., with an emphasis on social change. Curbstne Press, 321 Jackson St., Willimantic, CT 06220. Tel. (860) 423-5100. http://www.connix.com/-curbston/

Brujula is a bilingual magazine devoted to Latino literature in the U.S. Contact the editor at *Brujula*, Latin American Writers Institute, Hostos Community College, 500 Grand Concourse, Bronx, N.Y. 10451. Tel. (718) 518-4195.

Notes on Contributors

Originally from the Dominican Republic, **Julia Alvarez** emigrated to the U.S. with her parents at the age of ten. She is the author of three novels, *How the García Girls Lost Their Accents, In the Time of the Butterflies,* and *¡Yo!,* as well as two books of poems, *Homecoming* and *The Other Side.* Alvarez has taught creative writing to students and teachers at all levels. She now teaches literature and creative writing at Middlebury College.

Carol Bearse has worked as a Poet-in-the-Schools, and has taught all grades K–college. The former Director of the Magnet Writing Program at the Kane School, Bearse is currently the Literacy Specialist for the Fuller Middle School in Framingham, Massachusetts. Her poetry has appeared in *The Christian Science Monitor,* and most recently in *The Unitarian Universalist Poets: A Contemporary Survey* (Pudding House Press). She has given workshops for NCTE and IRA, and has published articles in *The Reading Teacher* and *The Whole Language Teachers Newsletter.* Her essay is part of a larger work in progress on the teaching of writing in middle school.

Deborah Cummins is a poet, fiction writer, and teacher. She received a James B. Michener Fellowship in Fiction and a Donald Barthelme Memorial Fellowship at the University of Houston, where she received her MFA. Cummins has conducted workshops for students and teachers of all grade levels, at the University of Chicago, Columbia College (Chicago), and Northwestern University, and for the Illinois Arts Council. In 1996 her novel manuscript took first place in the Washington Prize in Fiction.

Martín Espada is the author of five poetry collections, most recently *City of Coughing and Dead Radiators* and *Imagine the Angels of Bread* (Norton). He is also the editor of *Poetry Like Bread: Poets of the Political Imagination* (Curbstone), and the co-translator of *The Blood That Keeps Singing: Selected Poems* by Clemente Soto Vélez. Among Espada's many awards are two NEA Fellowships and the PEN/Revson Fellowshop. He is an Associate Professor in the English Department at the University of Massachusetts-Amherst.

Kate Farrell is a poet who has taught poetry writing to students of all ages. With Kenneth Koch, she produced two anthologies of poetry, *Sleeping on the Wing* and *Talking to the Sun.* The Metropolitan Museum of Art published her two other anthologies, *Art & Love* and *Art & Nature.* Also an actress, Farrell is a founding member of the New York Art Theatre Institute. Her poetry has appeared in *Poetry, Partisan Review, New York Arts Journal,* and other magazines.

Mary Sue Galindo is a liberal arts graduate from the University of Texas at Austin and received her teaching and bilingual certificates from Laredo State University. Sponsored by the Texas Commission on the Arts, she has taught creative writing in the schools and in economically depressed areas through the artist-in-education program and Project Bridge. Galindo lives in Laredo, Texas.

Kenneth Koch has published many books of poetry, drama, fiction, and criticism, as well as three classics on writing poetry, *Wishes, Lies, and Dreams, Sleeping on the Wing,* and *Rose, Where Did You Get That Red?* His most recent books of poetry are *One Train* and *On the Great Atlantic Rainway: Selected Poems 1950–1988* (Knopf). He has won numerous awards, including the Bollingen and Bobbitt prizes. He is Professor of English at Columbia University.

William Bryant Logan has published numerous translations of the work of Federico García Lorca, including *Once Five Years Pass and Other Dramatic Works.* In 1983 he received a grant from the National Endowment for the Humanities to translate three plays by Pedro Calderón de la Barca. He has taught poetry writing in the schools, and currently is poet-in-residence at St. John the Divine in New York City.

Julio Marzán holds a Ph.D. in Latin American literature from New York University and an MFA in Poetry from Columbia University. He is the author of *Translations without Originals,* a volume of poetry, and *The Spanish American Roots of William Carlos Williams,* a critical study. He is the editor of *Inventing the Word: An Anthology of Twentieth-Century Puerto Rican Poetry.* Marzán is Associate Professor of English at Nassau Community College.

David Mills received an M.A. in Poetry from New York University. He has taught poetry and playwriting in schools and prisons since 1990. In 1993 he received the BRIO Award for poetry. His writing has appeared in *Downbeat, The Village Voice, Essence,* and other periodicals. His play *The Serpent and the Dove* was produced by the Juilliard School of Drama.

Naomi Shihab Nye has been a visiting writer in the schools since 1974. Her anthologies of poems for young readers include *I Feel a Little Jumpy around You* (Simon & Schuster) and *This Same Sky* (Simon & Schuster). Her own books of poems are *Red Suitcase* (BOA Editions) and *Words under the Words: Selected Poems* (Far Corner Books). Her essays are collected in *Never in a Hurry* (University of South Carolina).

Ron Padgett is a poet, translator, and teacher. His most recent book of poetry is *New & Selected Poems* (Godine). His translations include *The Poet Assassinated and Other Stories* (North Point Press) by Guillaume Apollinaire and *Complete Poems* by Blaise Cendrars (University of California). His books on education include *Creative Reading* (NCTE) and *The Handbook of Poetic Forms*, published by Teachers & Writers Collaborative, where he is publications director. He also teaches Imaginative Writing at Columbia University.

Rosemarie Roqué has taught poetry to kids in New York City through Poets in Public Service and Columbia University's Summer Program for High School Students, and to adults in the Evening Program at the University of Iowa. Her poems have been published in *Sonora Review, Great Stream Review, The Journal, Santa Clara Review,* and some other magazines. She is currently a medical student at SUNY Stony Brook.

Suzann Steele Saltzman has Master's degrees in both Education and Humanities. A former fellow in the National Writing Project at the University of California-Davis, she currently teaches English at a college preparatory school in Dallas.

John Oliver Simon worked for California Poets in the Schools for twenty years and taught bilingual fifth and sixth grades at La Escuelita in Oakland, California. His poems in Spanish, *Son caminos*, was published by Hotel Ambos Mundos Press in Mexico City.

Mark Statman's poetry, fiction and criticism have appeared in *notus, Transfer, Pacific Review, Cover, Democracy & Education, Teachers & Writers, Rethinking Schools, The Nation,* and *The Village Voice,* as well as in *Old Faithful, The T&W Guide to Walt Whitman,* and *The T&W Handbook of Poetic Forms.* Statman has received fellowships from the NEA and the National Writers Project, as well as the Gold Key from the Columbia Press Association. He teaches Writing and Literature and Education Studies at Eugene

Lang College at the New School for Social Research and has worked in the schools for Teachers & Writers since 1985.

David Unger is a Guatemalan-born writer and translator. Currently he is the U.S. coordinator of the Guadalajara International Book Fair. The editor of Nicanor Parra's *Antipoems: New and Selected*, his most recent translations appear in *Small Hours of the Night: Selected Poems of Roque Dalton.*

Janine Pommy Vega has taught in bi-lingual programs in upstate New York schools and the New York City school system since 1976. She has conducted writing workshops for migrant workers in Genesco, New York, and the inmates of Lurigancho Prison, in Lima, Peru. She has performed her own work in Spanish throughout Colombia and Peru.

OTHER T&W BOOKS YOU MIGHT ENJOY

El Libro de la Escritura by Pingüino Tinto. The *only* poetry writing workbook in Spanish for young people. Includes 15 exciting writing exercises, a bibliography, and more.

The Teachers & Writers Handbook of Poetic Forms, edited by Ron Padgett. This T&W bestseller includes 74 entries on traditional and modern poetic forms by 19 poet-teachers. "A treasure"—*Kliatt.* "The definitions not only inform, they often provoke and inspire. A small wonder!"—*Poetry Project Newsletter.* "An entertaining reference work"—*Teaching English in the Two-Year College.* "A solid beginning reference source"—*Choice.*

Poetry Everywhere: Teaching Poetry Writing in School and in the Community by Jack Collom & Sheryl Noethe. This big and "tremendously valuable resource work for teachers" (*Kliatt*) at all levels contains 60 writing exercises, extensive commentary, and 450 examples.

The Adventures of Dr. Alphabet by Dave Morice presents 104 amusing and imaginative poetry writing methods that have excited his students for two decades. "Teachers and parents will treasure this collection"—*School Enrichment Model Network News.*

The List Poem: A Guide to Teaching & Writing Catalog Verse by Larry Fagin defines list poetry, traces its history, gives advice on teaching it, offers specific writing ideas, and presents more than 200 examples by children and adults. An *Instructor* poetry pick. "Outstanding"—*Kliatt.*

The T&W Guide to Walt Whitman edited by Ron Padgett. The first and only guide to teaching the work of Walt Whitman from K–college. "A lively, fun, illuminating book"—Ed Folsom, editor of *The Walt Whitman Quarterly.*

Educating the Imagination, Vols. 1 & 2, edited by Christopher Edgar and Ron Padgett. A big selection of the best articles from 17 years of *Teachers & Writers* magazine, with ideas and assignments for writing poetry, fiction, plays, history, folklore, parodies, and much more.

Old Faithful: 18 Writers Present Their Favorite Writing Assignments, edited by Christopher Edgar and Ron Padgett. A collection of sure-fire exercises in imaginative writing for all levels, developed and tested by veteran writing teachers.

Personal Fiction Writing by Meredith Sue Willis. A complete and practical guide for teachers of writing from elementary through college level. Contains more than 340 writing ideas. "A terrific resource for the classroom teacher as well as the novice writer"—*Harvard Educational Review.*

~

For a complete free T&W publications catalogue, contact
Teachers & Writers Collaborative
5 Union Square West, New York, NY 10003–3306
tel. (212) 691-6590.
Visit our World Wide Web site at http://www.twc.org